• HALSGROVE DISCOVER SERIES ➤

Charles Dickens

Rediscovering the places & characters portrayed in his books

STEPHEN BROWNING

HALSGROVE

First published in Great Britain in 2012

Copyright © Stephen Browning 2012

British Library Cataloguing-in-Publication Data
A CIP record for this title is available from the British Library

ISBN 978 0 85704 126 5

HALSGROVE
Halsgrove House,
Ryelands Business Park,
Bagley Road, Wellington, Somerset TA21 9PZ
Tel: 01823 653777   Fax: 01823 216796
email: sales@halsgrove.com

Part of the Halsgrove group of companies
Information on all Halsgrove titles is available at: www.halsgrove.com

Printed in Italy by Grafiche Flaminia

Contents

Dedication

I SEE A 12 YEAR OLD BOY buying pudding in the Strand. His father – the shame! – is in prison for debt. I look up again and see a 22 year old wandering the streets of London in a state of such happiness that he cannot talk to anyone as his first article has been accepted by a publisher. Just two years later this young writer is rapidly becoming a major literary star with the incredible success of *The Pickwick Papers*. Then I see some of the greatest novels in the English language tumbling, one after another from the pen of this amazing man. His name, as all the world now knows, is Charles Dickens.

It is now two hundred years since his birth on 7 February 1812. He would be delighted to know that today he is loved more than ever.

Happy Birthday, Charles!

Image Credits

Juliet Browning, images on pages 9, 102, 104, 126, 127, 128, 129, 130. Daniel Tink, images on pages 18, 30, 79, 80, 81, 84, 85, 86, 101, 103, 105, 106, 119, 122 (top 2). David A Berwick and Anne M. May, images on pages 91, 92, 93, 94. Mark Staples, images on pages 112 (bottom) 123, 124, 125. Mark is the author of *Portrait of Suffolk* (Halsgrove) and is copyright holder of images accredited in the text. see www.markstaples.co .uk All other original images, Stephen Browning.

Special Acknowledgements

Thanks to my sister, Juliet, for proof reading much of the text and also for taking some of the photographs, particularly of Cornwall, Guildford and Chichester. You have always been there for me. Kid brothers are meant to be a pain the neck, aren't they? I have tried hard to fulfil expectations.

As ever, I am grateful to my friend and co-author on many literary and photographic adventures, Daniel Tink, for the specially commissioned pictures of the West End of London. We have had lots of fun on this, and previous, books. Thanks for providing brilliant images of London, Great Yarmouth and Cornwall.

Eminent Norfolk historian, David A. Berwick, has been unstinting in his help, as he has for several other publications. In particular, he and Anne M. May most generously volunteered to take time out of their very busy choral schedule to take some pictures of Greta Bridge and surrounding countryside, a 'must' for any Dickens' fan. David and Anne were very grateful to Lady Dorothy Gilbertson who now lives in what was, in Dickens' time, The George Hotel. Lady Dorothy allowed access to her home and gardens – the picture of Greta Bridge was taken from the bottom of her garden.

Also, grateful acknowledgement to Professor Ming-Yu Tseng, Professor of Linguistics at National Sun Yat-Sen University in the beautiful country of Taiwan. Ming-yu is a linguist and has taken me to task many times, the text being much the better for this.

Thanks also to Mark Staples who has permitted me to use some of the images from his superb book *Portrait of Suffolk* (Halsgrove).

Imperial College provided ideal accommodation for my researches in London. Some parts of this account were written in my room there overlooking The Royal College of Music to the faint strains of clarinet and piano.

Gad's Hill Place, my favourite website on all things Dickens, has helped me with images.

Finally, thanks to Simon Butler of Halsgrove who, having listened to my enthusiasms for Dickens many times over lunch, suggested this book.

Introduction

I REALLY HOPE YOU will enjoy this book.

If you already are familiar with the work of Charles Dickens, I look forward to sharing my enthusiasms with you. If you are new to the greatest of our English novelists, I hope you will find this book a welcoming and happy introduction.

Dickens was above all else an entertainer. He was not overly-concerned with plot structure or even the language he was using provided he made his point effectively. He also wanted to be a friend, a sort of kindly uncle, who could both help make the reader feel warmly involved, and strike a blow for a better world.

The idea of this book is to take a look at the places associated with him, both in real life and in his novels, short stories and magazine articles. It can also be used as a walking tour in some cases. It has not always been possible – you can hardly, for example, just nip over the sea from Portsmouth to the Isle of Wight – but some areas are perfect should you wish to take some exercise. Chapters 2, 4, 5, 6,7, and 8 are designed as walks for those who wish to tread exactly the same streets as Dickens himself. However, this is not necessary as I have included as many photographs and pictures as I could, and hopefully you can also see everything well in your 'mind's eye' while sitting in a familiar and comfortable armchair.

So, let's go to Rochester! I will explain why as we go…

Stephen
Norwich 2012

1
Rochester – the beginning and the end

Early Life. Portsmouth. Debt and Prison. Warren's Blacking Factory. Chatham and Rochester. Gad's Hill Place. The Cathedral. The Pickwick Papers. *The Mystery of Edwin Drood.* Queen Victoria. The End.

Birthplace (first floor) of Charles Dickens at Mile End, Portsmouth.

FOR CHARLES DICKENS, Rochester was both the beginning and the end.

True, he had been born in Mile End on the outskirts of Portsmouth on 7 February 1812, seven years after the Battle of Trafalgar and three years before the final defeat of Napoleon at Waterloo. It was a Friday, the same day as his 'favourite child', David Copperfield, was born, and a day that was always special to him. His father, John, who worked for the Naval Pay Office, was a friendly and gregarious chap, good-looking by all accounts, and always had his brain attuned to what we would today call 'upward mobility'. He liked to buy books about a new town or area whenever he moved, which was often – maybe he read them or maybe they were to show a commitment to his new friends and neighbours. Elizabeth, Charles' Mother, was 23, and shared her husband's taste for 'society' – indeed, she is reported to have attended a ball on the eve of the birth. Charles already had a sister of eighteen months, Fanny.

The seeds of the later shame and insecurity, neither of which Charles Dickens could ever shake off no matter how famous or rich he became, are already laid out. John, wanting more than anything to be 'respectable', tempted and unable to resist spending more than a relatively humble clerk earned, and having to go wherever his paymasters dictated, was to end up in Marshalsea Prison for debt before young Charles was in his teens.

At twelve years old, Charles was sent to Warren's Blacking Factory where his dreams of becoming a gentlemen seemed lost forever amongst the rats flooding into Hungerford Stairs from the adjacent River Thames. But even more importantly for this young boy was the unfathomable shame and pain of it all. He was a very sensitive boy and was most upset when he gained the nickname 'the little gentleman' from his young workmates. He had one good friend, however, called Fagin, though why this lad's name ended up

Above left: Dickens' birthplace as it is today.

Above right: A view of the main dockyard gates today – John Dickens worked in the Pay Office just inside.

Left: HMS *Victory* at Portsmouth dockyard. Charles Dickens was born seven years after the Battle of Trafalgar and this ship would have been the toast of the nation and still very much in active service. It was finally moved here in 1922. Although very much in awe of the sea – Scrooge flies over it and Steerforth is destroyed by it – it is perhaps surprising that more of his storylines do not feature life on the ocean.

A Fred Barnard drawing of young David Copperfield in despair at the Blacking Warehouse.

Right: The Blacking Factory would have stood close to where the Embankment underground station now stands.

appended to the premier villain in *Oliver Twist*, is a mystery. Maybe it is because not all of Fagin is villainous and this young man represented the kindly side, the side that shied away from the pure evil of Sikes. Whatever the reason, Dickens never enlightened us, but it is quite possible there was much more going on in the factory than the manufacture and bottling of boot polish. Physical and sexual exploitation was rife, and whilst he exposed the former whenever he could, Dickens always maintained a typical Victorian antipathy to discussing the latter.

In the morning and evening, Charles would visit his father in Marshalsea Prison. For some of this time he lived at Lant Street, a still-existing everyday street, just a few yards from the prison. His father is reputed to have given him a lecture on finance on one of these visits, which would later be utilized in Micawber's immortal lines: '*Annual income twenty pounds, annual expenditure nineteen pounds nineteen and six, result happiness. Annual income twenty pounds, annual expenditure twenty pounds ought and six, result misery.*' I don't expect, though, that this went down terribly well at the time.

Far left: Lant Street today. The pub 'The Glad' is named after William Gladstone, twice Chancellor of the Exchequer in Dickens' lifetime and Prime Minister for the first time (of four) two years before Dickens' death. By coincidence, both men shared a sympathy for the downtrodden, including prostitutes, Gladstone himself getting into a bit of hot water about this later in his career.

Left: All that remains of Marshalsea Prison is this wall (right) which now forms part of an alleyway alongside the churchyard of St George's Church in Borough High Street.

Message in stone alongside present-day Marshalsea Prison.

The Park that houses gravestones of former prisoners. The wall to the left is that of the Marshalsea.
Inset: In the churchyard of St George's Church, now a peaceful park, are these gravestones of some inmates of the Marshalsea.

Just off Borough High Street is Little Dorrit Court and Little Dorrit Playground.

Little Dorrit was baptized and married in St George's Church, which nowadays has the indignity of competing for the view with the new London skyscraper, 'The Shard'.

Dickens never liked to acknowledge this period of his life, but he wrote of it as fiction in *David Copperfield*. The legacy – insecurity, fear of debt and the perceived need to never stop working at a pace few other mortals could match for even a short time, was to hasten his premature death. No matter how much applause he received, in both England and America, it could ever make him feel secure and content. This is a constant throughout his life and can be traced back to his earliest years. No Peace. No Rest. No Tranquility. '*If my Father had not died,*' Mamie Dickens wrote about that fateful June afternoon in 1870, fifty-eight years after Charles' arrival in a first floor Portsmouth bedroom just before midnight '*he would have gone insane*'.

The Dickens family moved several times in the early years and, in April 1817, they were posted to Chatham which merges with the historic town of Rochester. Charles was five.

Chatham is not writ large in Dickens' work. However, it does have the distinction of being the model for Mudfog which features in *The Mudfog Papers*, serialized in *Bentley's Miscellany* when Dickens was 25 years old. This is a piece of youthful literary slapstick, maybe not as subtle as his later work but extremely funny. It follows the proceedings of '*The Mudfog Society for the Advancement of Everything*', a parody of *The British Society for the Advancement of Science* which had been set up in 1831. Although this particular society has become extremely respected, it was at the time just one of many which were set up by the high-minded Victorians for the advancement of just-about-everything and it was a target that the youthful high spirits of Dickens could not resist taking a shot at.

In literary terms, Rochester – a little way along the very same street as Chatham – is the famous town to which the Pickwick Club came for its first adventure. Dickens was 24 and, before the book, published in monthly parts, was anywhere near finished, he was a major and permanent star in the literary firmament.

'Pickwick' was actually born of tragedy in that the original and brilliant illustrator, Robert Seymour, blew his brains out after a few episodes. '*Sketches By Boz*', discussed in Chapter 4, had been enough of a success to persuade Chapman & Hall, the publishers, that the young Charles might possibly contribute to the project. The vision was initially to create illustrations about sporting life with explanatory words, but upon Seymour's death, Dickens succeeded in having this reversed – henceforth his writing would be the main feature and the drawings would back up his text. Dickens knew next-to-nothing about sport and so we only very reluctantly and occasionally find Mr Pickwick – who also went from thin to portly at this time – and his three companions, Messrs Tracy Tupman, Augustus Snodgrass and Nathaniel Winkle, indulging in exercise. Dickens is rarely inadvertently funny, but his lack of understanding of the rules of cricket, in a scene at Dingley Dell, will bring a chuckle to lovers of the game. He didn't know his square cut from his fine leg.

The hustle and bustle of the Thames today. Dickens would have crossed near this spot many times in order to see his father in Marshalsea Prison. The great 'black dome' of St Paul's became a symbol of hope in his novels.

The little graveyard by the North Door of Rochester cathedral : Dickens said he would like to be buried here.

The Pickwick Papers was initially only a very minor success. At first, monthly sales struggled to reach 500. When Dickens introduced Sam Weller as Mr Pickwick's worldly-savvy but golden-hearted manservant, sales shot up to the tens of thousands. There is almost no predicament, one feels, that the unworldly but kind Mr Pickwick can get himself into that the canny young Sam – aided by his father sometimes – cannot get him out of. Early shades of Jeeves and Wooster. Part of the fun, bearing in mind that readers had to wait a month to find the outcome, was trying to work out 'how on earth is Sam going to do it this time?'

Although Rochester and the surrounding area became the scenes of high spirits and good-natured farce in the book, the Cathedral is treated in a special way. It was dark and earthy, the pathways worn down by pilgrim's feet. During a subsequent visit many years later, Dickens confided to his friend and first biographer, John Forster, that he wanted his mortal remains to be placed in the little Cathedral graveyard (it very nearly happened).

He continues the 'musty' theme in his last, unfinished novel, *The Mystery of Edwin Drood*. The joyous and often unthinking effervescence of youth has given way here to an atmosphere of wordliness, exotic mystery, opium, febrile mortality and shadows. Rochester has the altogether more sombre name of Cloisterham ('cloisters': things hidden and shut in, secret corners, old cold stone, people shuffling silently by). The Cathedral, too, looms darker. The writing, within days of his own death, is exquisite: ' *Old Time heaved a mouldy sigh from tomb and arch and vault; and gloomy shadows began to deepen in corners; and damps began to rise from green patches of stone; and jewels, cast upon the pavement of the nave from stained glass by the declining sun, began to perish…*'

In the non-literary world Rochester was also there for Dickens at the beginning and the end of his all-too-short life. When he was growing up there were two worlds – the cash-strapped, permanently-on-the-edge-of-the-financial-precipice one of his father, and the other a dream existence. One day he went for a carriage ride with his Father on the Gravesend Road and came across a house called Gad's Hill Place. He fell in love with this seeming 'mansion' straight away. We find the following in '*The Uncommercial Traveller*':

"*Bless you, sir,' said the very queer small boy, 'when I was not more than half as old as nine, it used to be a treat for me to be brought to look at it. And now, I am nine, I come by myself to look at it. And ever since I can recollect, my father, seeing me so fond of it, has often said to me, 'if you were to be very persevering and were to work hard, you might some day come to live in it.' 'Though that's impossible!' said the very queer small boy, drawing a low breath, and now staring at the house out of the window with all his might.*"

The house had been built in 1780 for the Mayor of Rochester, Thomas Stephens. When it came on to the market in 1856, Dickens bought it. He had the study equipped to his taste and humour: some dummy books were installed with titles such as *History of a Short Chancery Suit* and *Hansard's Guide to Refreshing Sleep*. A wooden Swiss chalet, a gift from actor Charles Fechter was erected in the garden. Many of the greatest novels were crafted here, including *Great Expectations*, *Our Mutual Friend* and his unfinished last, *The Mystery of Edwin Drood*. Otherwise, he used the study in the house itself.

Dickens' wooden chalet is now in a parlous state and has been transferred to the gardens of Eastgate House. It is supported inside by metal struts. A campaign to raise £100,000 to restore it is currently underway.

Great Ormond Street Hospital, London has a very special connection. In 2008, the desk and chair from Gad's Hill Place were sold for £433,250 and all the money given to Great Ormond Street Hospital for sick children. Dickens had spoken at the first fundraising dinner held at St Martin-in-the-Fields, London, two years after moving into Gad's Hill Place. He supported the hospital all his life. At first there were ten beds only; by 1880 the hospital helped 1690 in-patients and 19,000 out-patients, mostly drawn from the omnipresent slums.

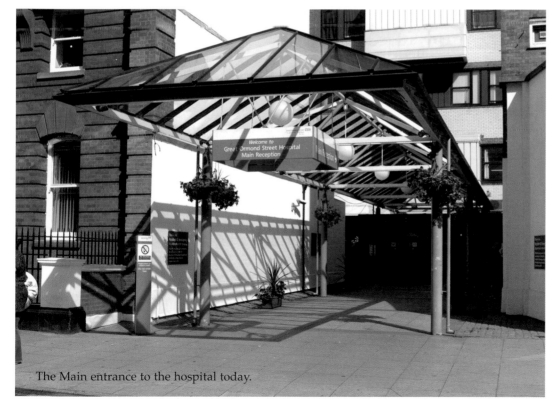

The Main entrance to the hospital today.

Great Ormond Street has become the world's finest children's hospital. Dickens would be amazed and delighted.

The House now forms part of a private school. 2012 sees the original house become a museum and heritage centre as the school will move into new buildings on the site. Dickens' great-great granddaughter, Marion Dickens, is a governor at the school.

Mamie Dickens, in *My Father as I Recall Him*, a wonderful, uncritical and loving portrait, gives detailed descriptions of the family life, games, meals and festivities that took place in this house. She writes that he had never been happier, although he was becoming severely worn down by this time, than during the last two years of his life. He kept up a hectic schedule. If he was alone with his family he would spend the day writing in the chalet before coming in for dinner, often at first withdrawn and quiet but soon gathering his spirits for games, a walk or sometimes correspondence afterwards. If he had guests, which was often, they had to abide by 'house rules' which included a certain amount of time working at something serious before frivolities began. Poor Wilkie Collins, although sixteen years his junior, was never particularly energetic and is reported to have tried to 'bunk off' to the library for a mid-morning cigar only to be brought to book and charged with a serious undertaking as mornings were apparently for work!

Albeit in fine spirits, Dickens could not stop the premature aging that was the inevitable result of his frenetic workload and, in particular, his public readings, in London and all over, to an invariably adoring public. Many people would come just to see this very famous man whose writing had helped shape their opinions and attitudes. Oftentimes, folk could not get into the venues. Inside, there would be silence as Dickens finished acting out the murder of Nancy in *Oliver Twist* or maybe, another favourite, Mr Pickwick's trial scene. Then the prolonged stomping and cheering would begin and an exhausted Dickens would come back on to the stage, tears streaming down his face.

Why did he do it? For adoration, certainly. The press fell over itself in its praise: *"Hear Dickens and die;"* trumpeted *The Scotsman, "you will never live to hear anything of its kind so good."* But also, for the money – the readings, increasingly against the advice of his doctor, were very lucrative and Dickens had convinced himself that he could never relax financially. The spectre of Marshalsea Prison was never to leave him alone and it has to be

'Charles Dickens in his study at Gad's Hill' by Samuel Hollyer.

Dickens and party pose in the porch of Gad's Hill Place. He liked nothing better than to have a full house when days would be spent in a mixture of work and play.

said that some of his ten children, along with his father, would not leave him alone financially either.

In March 1870 Dickens had an audience with the Queen. His left hand was swollen, he had a gammy foot and blurred vision. It was clear where he was heading. He had to stand during the audience but he was addressing one of his greatest fans. If only Victoria's beloved Disraeli had been present, as he well could have been, we should have had the three most powerful figures of the Victorian age in one room. Nonetheless, if we could each be granted one scene in which we could travel back in time, where we could be a 'fly on the wall', this occasion would be my request. Apparently, when other folk could hear, they talked of mundane things, including the price of food. But what when the doors were closed? Surely, now or before, Charles would have been offered a Knighthood or more? He was, after all the hero of his age, and had in very effective ways carried on the work of the revered late Prince Albert in promoting better education and working conditions for the common man. We have never been told, but it is entirely in keeping with his 'street cred' that the great man would have wanted to remain just plain 'Charles Dickens'.

On 8 June, Dickens wrote his last chapter. Almost his last words are of Rochester and are very bright, but how strange he should be thinking of the Resurrection and the Life and cold stone tombs warmed by the life-giving sun. The next day he would be dead.

'A brilliant morning shines on the old city. Its antiquities and ruins are surpassingly beautiful, with a lusty ivy gleaming in the sun, and the rich trees waving in the balmy air. Changes of glorious light from moving boughs, songs of birds, scents from gardens, woods, and fields—or, rather, from the one great garden of the whole cultivated island in its yielding time—penetrate into the Cathedral, subdue its earthy odour, and preach the Resurrection and the Life. The cold stone tombs of centuries ago grow warm; and flecks of brightness dart into the sternest marble corners of the building, fluttering there like wings.'

He had, according to his daughter, Mamie, had a fine lunch that day and smoked a cigar. He retired to his chalet, where the sentences above were written, until about an hour before dinner. Prior to food being served he wrote a couple of letters in his study. Once at the table, however, he looked poorly and admitted that he had been 'very ill' for about an hour. His speech became slurred and it was suggested he lie down. 'Yes, on the ground,' he said. He never recovered consciousness. At ten past six in the early evening of 9 June a tear welled up in his right eye and fell down his cheek. He was gone.

Rochester Cathedral lost him at the last. He was to have been buried there but his family were asked if they would prefer him to lie in Westminster Abbey. To this they agreed, provided the service was, as Dickens had previously instructed, carried out without fuss or ostentation.

Westminster Abbey claimed Dickens in the end.

2
Rochester on foot and Cooling Church

The High Street. Clock. Bull Inn. Guildhall. College Gate. Eastgate House. Pumblechook and Sapsea. Satis House. Cooling Church. Magwitch. Picnic.

WHEN YOU ARE A CHILD, everything seems very big, doesn't it? Then when you revisit a place it can be with a sense of disappointment.

Rochester certainly changed in Dickens' perception. When he was a young boy, the High Street, Castle, Cathedral and surrounding marshes and lanes constituted a vast magical kingdom. When he returned, while writing an article for *The Uncommercial Traveller* some years later, the High Street had 'shrunk fearfully' and the 'finest clock in the world' was just another 'inexpressive' clock. The town had become 'Dulsborough'. Later, as we say earlier, it was to become the slightly menacing 'Cloisterham'.

'The finest clock in the world' or just another 'inexpressive' clock?

The town always maintained a hold on his imagination, though. Several of the locations, discussed below, are used more than once in his work, sometimes transported 'lock, stock and barrel', to another part of the kingdom. It was also the last place he was seen alive by the public, on 6 June 1870, leaning against a fence opposite Satis House, 'casing the joint' in his imagination; and we can only guess that it would have been pressed into service for a third time in the final novel, *The Mystery of Edwin Drood*.

In 1836, as he was starting the book that was to propel him to youthful fame and fortune, it was the perfect place for Mr Pickwick and his readers to begin their wonderful adventures. It can never lose this distinction.

There was to be a military parade:

'The whole population of Rochester and the adjoining towns rose from their beds at an early hour of the following morning, in a state of the utmost bustle and excitement. A grand review was to take place upon the lines.'

The magical Castle.

Needless to say, things did not go well. Mr Pickwick and friends somehow or other manage to place themselves directly in line as the soldiers, bayonets fixed, charge:

'Man is but mortal; and there is a point beyond which human courage cannot extend. Mr Pickwick gazed through his spectacles for an instant on the advancing mass, and then fairly turned his back and – we will not say fled; firstly because it is an ignoble term, and, secondly, because Mr Pickwick's figure was by no means adapted for that mode of retreat – he trotted away, at as quick a rate as his legs would convey him; so quickly, indeed, that he did not perceive the awkwardness of his situation, to the full extent, until too late.'

Mr Pickwick is unceremoniously upended, and his boots *'elevated in air'*.

The Chairman of The Pickwick Club retreated to the comfort of the Bull Inn to recuperate. This fine old inn has an illustrious real and literary history. Before she became Queen, in 1826, Victoria stayed here, as did Dickens himself on several occasions. It also appears in *Great Expectations* as The Blue Boar. Young Pip uses the place as he pursues his promising prospects. Alas, when word gets out that his great expectations have disappeared, he is not as well received there as he would have hoped. Worldly common sense, though, which he has been severely lacking until that point, is beginning to dawn:

'It was evening when I arrived, much fatigued by the journey I had so often made so easily. The Boar could not put me up in my usual bedroom, which was engaged (probably by some one who had expectations), and could only assign me a very indifferent chamber among the pigeons and

The mighty river curves around Rochester Castle today – but the boats are all pleasure craft, not the naval ships that Dickens would have seen.

Above: The wonderful flowers of the Catalpa Tree can be seen in July and August.

Above left: The Cathedral, looking towards the West Door. The magnificent tree is a very rare Catalpa Tree, sometimes called the American Indian Bean Tree, and is over 100 years old.

Satis House. The home of Miss Havisham in *Great Expectations*. It is also across the road that Dickens was last seen alive three days before his death, leaning on a fence and gazing at the house.

21

Many modern day traders in Rochester High Street have ingeniously utilized words associated with Dickens in their business names.

This old Inn is probably both the Bull Inn in *The Pickwick Papers* and The Blue Boar in *Great Expectations*.

The Guildhall where Pip is apprenticed to Joe in *Great Expectations*.

post-chaises up the yard. But, I had as sound a sleep in that lodging as in the most superior accommodation the Boar could have given me, and the quality of my dreams was about the same as in the best bedroom.'

The Guildhall, where Pip was apprenticed in *Great Expectations*, is opposite the Bull.

Eastgate House in the High Street is an example of a setting that Dickens used in more than one novel. A genuine school for girls in Dickens' time, it serves as the Westgate Seminary for Young Ladies, scene of Mr Pickwick's comic misadventures in *The Pickwick*

Eastgate House.

This magnificent building was pressed into service twice, once as the home of Mr Sapsea and, earlier, that of Mr Pumblechook.

Papers. Rosa also attends Miss Twinkleton's school for young ladies, an identical building but transferred to Bury St Edmunds, in *The Mystery of Edwin Drood*. Here: *'Rosa soon made the discovery that Miss Twinkleton didn't read fairly. She cut the love-scenes, interpolated passages in praise of female celibacy, and was guilty of other pious frauds.'*

In the same way, the black and white timbered building opposite was both the home of 'the purest jackass in Cloisterham' in *The Mystery of Edwin Drood*, the Honourable Mayor, Mr Sapsea, and the appalling, smug hypocrite in *Great Expectations*, Mr Pumblechook. The latter is described by young Pip as '… *the torment, with his fishy eyes and mouth open, his sandy hair inquisitively on end…*' He inhabits the novel, in a lowish but infuriatingly irritating key, from first to last; this reader, at least, always hoping for a metaphorical giant fly swat to emerge from out of the sky to thwack him. The young Dickens resists and milks every groan and laugh possible from his presence, an example of his genius for inventing secondary characters that nearly steal the show.

Mr Pumblechook is relatively unimportant in the story. Some other 'non primary' characters in Dickens' novels are more rounded, with spheres of influence and power all their own; some, even, are key to important plot developments. Silas Wegg (*Our Mutual Friend*), The Artful Dodger (*Oliver Twist*), Uriah Heep (*David Copperfield*), Mrs Pipchin (*Dombey and Son*), Betsey Trotwood (*David Copperfield*), Bradley Headstone (*Our Mutual Friend*), Smike (*Nicholas Nickleby*) and, to my mind the greatest and funniest of them all, Mrs Gamp (*Martin Chuzzlewit*) – she who drinks gin out of a china teapot and has an imaginary friend, Mrs Harris, with whom she is in constant communication when half sozzled (which is most of the time) and who always has something very complimentary to say about her – and hundreds more, poured from Dickens' imagination to entertain and dazzle us.

Along the High Street, at the Crossroads at Northgate, is College Gate. This is the home to which Jasper struggles after having been *'took a little poorly'* in the cathedral following his stint in a London opium den in *The Mystery of Edwin Drood*. The Dean, Mr Tope and the Reverend Mr Crisparkle are concerned:

'They all three look towards an old stone gatehouse crossing the Close, with an arched thoroughfare passing beneath it. Through its latticed windows, a fire shines out upon the fast-darkening scene, involving in shadow the pendent masses of ivy and creeper covering the building's front. As the deep Cathedral-bell strikes the hour, a ripple of wind goes through these at their distance, like a ripple of the solemn sound that hums through tomb and tower, broken niche and defaced statue, in the pile close at hand.'

The second oldest cathedral in the UK beckons through the College Gate. Here it is as approached, in autumn:

'Not only is the day waning, but the year. The low sun is fiery and yet cold behind the monastery ruin, and the Virginia creeper on the Cathedral wall has showered half its deep red leaves down on the pavement. There has been rain this afternoon, and a wintry shudder goes among the little pools on the cracked, uneven flag-stones, and through the giant elm-trees as they shed a gust of tears.'

The rain as tears, shed for something undefined, is an image used elsewhere in Dickens. Later, in novels such as *Our Mutual Friend*, water, and, in particular, the Thames, represents life itself.

There is a very famous quote about looking down the crypt stairs in the Cathedral: *'it's like looking down the throat of Old Time.'*

Above: The incomparable Mrs Gamp, teapot with gin inside at the ready, by Fred Barnard 1870s.

Right: This is Jasper's house in *The Mystery of Edwin Drood*. He retired here having been 'took a little poorly' following his trip to a London opium den. Next door is the home of Mr Tope, verger at Rochester Cathedral. The last scene ever written by Dickens takes place in Mr Tope's kitchen.

25

Above left: Minor Canon Row

Above right: Vines Park, through which Pip walked to see Miss Havisham.

At the rear of the cathedral is a row of cottages, Minor Canon Row, which housed, in Dickens' day, some of the lesser clergy. They are referred to in *The Mystery of Edwin Drood*.

If you carry on walking, Vines Park hoves into view. Pip takes this route on his way to see Miss Havisham for the last time in *Great Expectations*. He would probably have been thinking of all his past pain – the desperate, unrequited, love for Estella, who had been brought up by Miss Havisham to break men's hearts. Maybe he was thinking of her cruel words: *'Moths, and all sorts of ugly creatures hover about a lighted candle. Can the candle help it?'*

Surely, too, he could have been wondering how he managed to keep his youthful sanity on his most significant previous visit. The lady of the house, jilted on her wedding day, had resolved to keep everything in one room exactly as it was at twenty to nine that fateful morning, at the precise moment she received the unforgiveable news of her lover's desertion and treachery. Pip, a young and innocent boy, in love with a girl who seems to despise him, is introduced to the rot and decay of the wedding room, in a scene of horror enough to send a sensitive nature over the edge. Pip is talking:

'The most prominent object was a long table with a tablecloth spread upon it, as if a feast had been in preparation when the house and the clocks all stopped together. An epergne or centerpiece of some kind was in the middle of this cloth; it was so heavily overhung with cobwebs that its form was quite indistinguishable; and, as I looked along the yellow expanse out of which I remember its seeming to grow, like a black fungus, I saw speckle-legged spiders with blotchy bodies running home to it, as if some circumstance of the greatest public importance had just transpired in the spider community…

"This," said she, pointing to the long table with her stick, "is where I will be laid when I am dead. They shall come and look at me here."'

Pip's last visit does, in fact, end with Miss Havisham's death. She catches her dress in the fire and dies of burns a short while later. She realizes that she has merely broken Pip's

FROM WHOM WE HAVE
GREAT EXPECTATIONS

At a time when there was no other media to seriously challenge the written word, a new monthly segment of a Dickens' novel was a major event indeed. Apart from anything else he was a one-man entertainment business and the public adored him.

'What have I done? What have I done?' Pip and Miss Havisham.

27

heart, ruined Estella's chances of happiness, and achieved nothing by her selfishness. She cries, *"What have I done? What have I done"*

If you drive a short way out of Rochester on the A228, or fancy a walk of about 12 miles from the Cathedral, you will come to the Church of Cooling. This is a very pretty little church and Dickens would often come here with his guests or by himself. It is famous as the setting for the opening scene of *Great Expectations* where a very young Pip is terrified out of his wits by the escaped convict, Magwitch:

'The man, after looking at me for a moment, turned me upside down, and emptied my pockets. There was nothing in them but a slice of bread. When the church came to itself – for he was so sudden and strong that he made it go head over heels before me, and I saw the steeple under my feet – when the church came to itself, I say, I was seated on a high tombstone, trembling, while he ate the bread ravenously.'

Title page of first edition of *Great Expectations*, 1861.

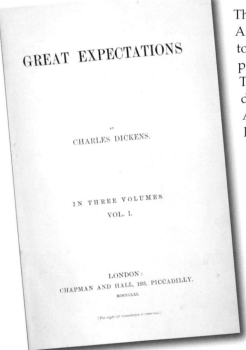

The small lozenge-shaped gravestones which Pip shows Magwitch as being the resting places of his mother and siblings are still there.

There is a well documented little story which illustrates Dickens' earthy humour. After a walk to the church with friends one fine day, Dickens selected a large flat tombstone in a corner of the churchyard. Here he spread out a white tablecloth and proceeded to unload the provisions the party had brought with them on to the cloth. Then, disappearing behind another tombstone, he sprang up a few moments later dressed as a head waiter and proceeded to attend assiduously to each of his guests. A couple of tramps walked by and he attended to them, too, making sure that they had all the food they needed.

The lonely spot, the performance, the generosity, the presence of death amongst the living, the hint of madness – it is all pure Dickens.

3
Dickens and London

Old Father Thames, the fog, rain and sea. The Bridges – Vauxhall, Westminster, Waterloo, Blackfriars, Southwark and London. Sikes meets his fate on Jacob's Island. Tears and redemption. The Law is a (very slow) ass. Water everywhere.

WAGS WILL TELL YOU that, today, London is inhabited by two types of people – those who act as if it is the centre of the universe and those who know it is. Dickens subscribed to the latter view. London imbues much of his writings, and often he was fascinated by the dirt and squalor of it all:

'It was a foggy day in London, and the fog was heavy and dark. Animate London, with smarting eyes and irritated lungs, was blinking, wheezing, and choking; inanimate London was a sooty spectre, divided in purpose between being visible and invisible, and so being wholly neither.'

Our Mutual Friend

Even the rain cannot wash the city clean:

'In the country, the rain would have developed a thousand scents, and every drop would have had its bright association with some beautiful form of growth or life. In the city, it developed only foul stale smells, and was a sickly, lukewarm, dirt-stained wretched addition to the gutters.'

Little Dorrit

The Artful Dodger introduces Oliver Twist to Fagin , by George Cruikshank.

Through almost all his books flows a river. In London, which means in most of his great novels, there is, of course, the River Thames. My favourite example of Dickens' use of the river is in the opening chapter of *Our Mutual Friend* where Gaffer Hexham and his beautiful daughter Lizzie, search the river between Southwark and London Bridges for dead bodies whose pockets they can rob before claiming a reward. Lizzie's beauty, both physical and spiritual – Dickens like to put them both together and his females generally are either angels or harridans – as she rows the boat for her father, contrasts with the unremitting filth of the river and their gruesome task. The *Guardian* newspaper, on Tuesday 3 May 1864, in a review of the first installment of the work, while celebrating the fact that *'for some time to come there will be a new interest in the first of each month, for a new novel by Dickens is a literary event'*, comments that *'Mr Dickens' old horror of the dark river comes out again in the very first sentences.'*

This area was transformed during Dickens' lifetime. The Palace of Westminster, as seen here, was begun in 1840 and construction lasted 30 years. Westminster Bridge was finally opened in 1862. The city he grew up in no longer existed by the time of his death.

It is interesting to compare Dickens' view of the city to the romantic view of Wordsworth, writing twenty years before Dickens took up his pen. Wordsworth found himself in a carriage temporarily held up on Westminster Bridge in the early morning. This, then would have been the romantic image Dickens grew up with:

Earth hath not anything to show more fair:
Dull would he be of soul who could pass by
A sight so touching in its majesty:
This City now doth, like a garment, wear
The beauty of the morning; silent, bare,
Ships, towers, domes, theatres and temples lie
Open unto the fields, and to the sky;
All bright and glittering in the smokeless air.

Never did sun more beautifully steep
In his first splendor, valley, rock, or hill;
Ne'er saw I, never felt, a calm so deep!
The river glideth at his own sweet will:
Dear God! The very houses seem asleep;
And all that mighty heart is lying still!

Nowadays, the Thames is wondrously cleaned up. Fish, which for decades have not been seen, now flourish right up to the city and beyond. There are over 120 species which thrive now, including the rare Twaite Shad which spawns in the tidal reaches. (The most unusual catch was a shark in the 18th century, in which was found a gold chain and various valuable items of jewellery, the unfortunate owner presumably having been digested). Brown shrimps and Chinese mitten crabs are thriving along the banks. Not so, when Dickens was writing. The Thames was lifeless, stinking of human excrement and all manner of filth. Just prior to the publication of *Our Mutual Friend* had been the summer of 'The Great Stink' when, in 1858, Parliament had had enough and adjourned business until the problem could be sorted. This pollution much to do with the introduction of flush toilets which, whilst reducing the 'cesspot' culture of the city whereby human and all other waste would just be thrown out on to the streets, actually made the Thames much worse by discharging everything into straight into it. There was no Embankment – this was one of the by-products of Joseph Bazalgette's miraculous and still functioning system of underground sewers – the buildings of London literally extended into the river.

Monument on the banks of the Thames to Joseph Bazalgette, responsible for building the still-functioning sewers after 'The Great Stink' of London.

The poorest classes lived by or above the water. Their cruel lives could be short – even much later, in 1905, Henry Mayhew's report into the poor found that, in the East End, the average length of life for 'men' was 16 years only. It was not surprising that people wondered if the river was responsible for producing deformed humanity, like the fearful Quilp in *The Old Curiosity Shop*:

'He ate hard eggs, shell and all, devoured gigantic prawns with the heads and tails on, chewed tobacco and watercress at the same time and with extraordinary greediness, drank boiling tea without winking, bit his fork and spoon till they bent again, and in short performed so many horrifying and uncommon acts that the women were nearly frightened out of their wits, and began to doubt if he were really a human creature.'

Most people today are aware of Jacob's Island, if not by name, at least by celluloid, as it is where Sikes meets his nasty end, and is a gift to film-makers. Dickens was very pleased to have discovered it (it lies in Bermondsey by today what is Wolseley Street), as it was just not somewhere that people even then frequented.

Jacob's Island in Dickens' time, by unknown artist.

Dickens may have found it as a result of a tour he undertook for human rights' activist, Angela Burdett-Coutts, while trying to determine the extent of prostitution in the capital. Many people, as a consequence of the terrific climax of *Oliver Twist*, still think of Victorian London like this: '*Near to that part of the Thames on which the church at Rotherhithe abuts, where the buildings on the banks are the dirtiest and the vessels on the river blackest with the dust of colliers and the smoke of close-built low-roofed houses, there exists the filthiest, the strangest, the most extraordinary of the localities that are hidden London, wholly unknown, even by name, to that great mass of its inhabitants.*'

The central part of the Thames had, in Dickens' day, several famous bridges. In order, coming up-river, they are: Vauxhall Bridge – Vauxhall Pleasure Gardens on the south side and Chelsea to the north; Westminster Bridge – Astley's famous circus to the south and Parliament to the north; Waterloo Bridge – very unsafe to the south with The Strand and Covent Garden to the north; Blackfriars Bridge – Fleet Street, Temple and St Paul's to the north; Southwark Bridge – Southwark Cathedral to the south and the City to the north; and London Bridge – The Marshalsea, Horsemonger and Kings Bench prisons to the south and Billingsgate to the north.

'Please, Sir, Can I have some more?' Illustration by George Cruikshank for *Oliver Twist*, 1837.

Dickens was fascinated by these bridges. Firstly, bridges symbolize passing from one area or state to another – in *Oliver Twist* they lead from Mr Brownlow's fine house in Pentonville to the filth and human degradation of Jacob's Island, where Sikes meets his maker. There is a clear implication, also, in Dickens' work, that good things happen north of the river and bad things generally south (many present day northern Londoners and taxi drivers of my acquaintance still hold this to be a self-evident truth). Thus there is also an unspoken assumption that crossing a bridge to the north, hopefully to live there, will also entail some degree of spiritual uplift.

Bridges can also be places of privileged neutrality, letting folk linger above the

Above left: In Dickens' times, south of the river was a generally dangerous and smelly place, the location for pleasure gardens and theatres of sometimes dubious repute. Now, you can walk from St Paul's straight across the Millennium Bridge to Tate Modern and the Royal Festival Hall. Many tourists, like this family here, cannot help turning round and snapping the view of St Paul's Cathedral from mid-way across the river. *Above right:* This is the inspiring view that the family in the adjoining picture, and thousands of others every day, will probably take home.

Below: Even today, down by the water's edge adjacent to London Bridge there are rickety muddy steps, and some slippery stone ones, too, leading down to the dirty-looking river, and it is not hard to imagine here a shivering and desperate Nancy waiting nervously for Mr Brownlow in *Oliver Twist*. For her pains, she would soon be bludgeoned to death by her lover, Sikes.

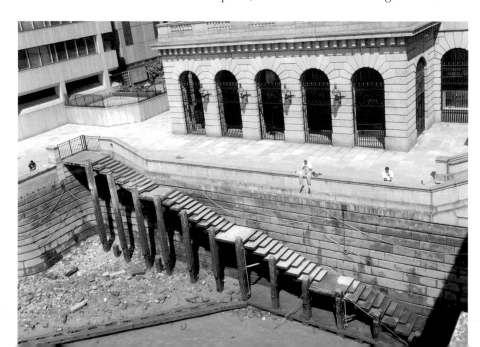

Southwark Bridge. This bridge was opened in 1921. It is often referred to as 'the metal bridge ' as opposed to 'the stone bridge', ie London Bridge. The previous Southwark Bridge, designed by John Rennie, features in *Little Dorrit* and *Our Mutual Friend*.

Barnaby in Newgate Gaol by Hablot Browne (Phiz).

unfathomable secrets of the river while they try to achieve a better life, or at least dream-on: in *Little Dorrit*, John proposes to Amy on Southwark Bridge. Or again, Jo, in *Bleak House*, takes a rest and gazes towards a great Dickensian symbol of hope, St Paul's Cathedral:

'*And there he sits, munching and gnawing, and looking up at the great Cross on the summit of St Paul's Cathedral, glittering above a red and violet-tinted cloud of smoke. From the boy's face one might suppose that sacred emblem to be, in his eyes, the crowning confusion of the great confused city; so golden, so high up, so far out of his reach. There he sits, the sun going down, the river running fast, the crowd flowing by him in two streams – everything moving on to some purpose and to one end – until he is stirred up, and told to "move on", too.*'

Then again, below the bridges nearer the river in a sort of 'nether world', twixt heaven above and death below, matters of great moment, such as Nancy's fateful meeting with Mr Brownlow down some cold, wet London Bridge steps, which led both to the murder of Nancy and the liberation of Oliver, are played out.

Sometimes bridges can just be fun as in *Barnaby Rudge* where the mob has a rare old time going backwards and forwards, first over one bridge then another, and back over the first, all to little effect, except for some of its members who are arrested and carted off to Newgate gaol (over yet another bridge).

One bridge Dickens did not have to write about was Tower Bridge as it was opened only in 1895. One can only savour the possible ways the fertile mind of Dickens may have used the hydraulic mechanism or the engine room – I have an image of Quilp, the evil dwarf-like villain referred to earlier, leaping across the opening sections of the bridge to escape his pursuers only to find one hand unavailingly clutching at the metalled road surface as the massive structure ground ever upwards, falling to his end in the filthy river water below. Or maybe, Sikes on one side of the opening road and Oliver on the other, with Sikes throwing a rope across to the young lad shouting for him to tie it round him and Sikes inadvertently slipping the rope around his neck before losing his footing and… yes, well, we must get on.

Rain, tears, rivers, fogs and mists, stagnant pools, the sea – all are omnipresent in his great novels. Thus we have the pure heaven-sent tears that young Paul Dombey cried when he himself was heaven-bound; the mighty ocean, over which Scrooge flies in *A Christmas Carol*, embracing *'secrets as profound as death'*; it is also at once the means of escape to a new life for the Micawbers in Australia and the ultimate arbiter for the flawed romantic hero,

Dolly Varden from *Barnaby Rudge*, painted in oils by William Powell Frith, 1842.

The world Dickens was not to see. Looking up-river from London Bridge in the 21st century we see Tower Bridge, opened after his death and in the far left hand corner, Canary Wharf, the city's latest financial centre – it is here that speculators and businessmen like Mr Dombey, or plain spendthrifts such as Lord Verisopht, nowadays travel to raise funds from the modern-day likes of Ralph Nickleby.

View from London Bridge, looking up to the
Monument – a little cleaner, maybe, than in
David Copperfield's time but, in important
respects, the same vista. David liked to stand
on the bridge and gaze up at the golden top
of the column. Dickens himself liked to
'people-watch' on London Bridge.

Fagin quivering in his condemned cell, as
drawn by George Cruikshank, 1838.

Steerforth, dying in a terrifying storm off Yarmouth after his fateful deeds in *David Copperfield;* Miss Havisham's tears for a wasted and cruel life in *Great Expectations* – water, water everywhere. Except, that is, for the arch-villains: Murdstone, Ralph Nickleby, Squeers, Jonas Chuzzlewit, Scrooge in his unreformed state, Quilp, Mr Dombey, Uriah Heep, Fagin (at least partially as he does a good deal of quivering and tearful wailing in his condemned cell, and I think Dickens maintained a soft spot in a small corner of his heart for him) – these men don't cry. For Dickens, shedding tears is an act of redemption and some characters he did not wish to redeem.

Dickens uses the metaphors of ships (not) sailing in his sustained attack on Chancery Lane and the Law in *Bleak House*: ' *It is the long vacation in the regions of Chancery Lane. The good ships Law and Equity, their tea-built, copper-bottomed, brazen-faced, and not by any means fast-sailing Clippers are laid up in ordinary. The Flying Dutchman, with a crew of ghostly clients imploring all they may encounter to peruse their papers, has drifted, for the time being, Heaven knows where... The Temple, Chancery Lane, Sergeant's Inn, and Lincoln's Inn even unto the Fields, are like tidal harbours at low water; where stranded proceedings, offices at anchor, idle clerks, lounging on lop-sided stools that will not recover their perpendicular until the current of Term sets in, lie high and dry upon the ooze of the long vacation.'*

In Dickens' novels, water is a symbol of life in all its complexities. In London, because of the Thames, it is omnipresent. As he wrote in *A Tale of Two Cities*, '*The water of the fountain ran, the swift river ran, the day ran into evening, so much life in the city ran into death according to rule, time and tide waited for no man, the rats were sleeping close together in their dark holes again...*'

London's newest bridge, only for pedestrians. The Millennium Bridge spans the river connecting St Paul's Cathedral and the Tate Modern.

Hungerford Stairs which led directly on to the stinking river – there was no embankment then. Dickens could hardly bear to mention the place and when he fictionalizes it in his 'favourite child', *David Copperfield*, it is transported up the river to Blackfriars where Warren's Blacking Factory is called 'Murdstone & Grinby's'. Murdstone was David's sadistic step-father, subsequently brought low to joyous effect by the formidable Aunt Betsey Trotwood. Murdstone had taken David out of school and told him he must henceforth earn his living. This again reflects real life as Charles' parents had money for just one child to be educated and they decided it was to be Fanny, his elder sister. Fiction sets Dickens free to express his pain: '…*I became, at ten years old, a little labouring hind in the service of Murdstone & Grinby's…*' He works with several other boys, including Mick Walker and one called Mealy Potatoes on account of his complexion.

'…*No words can express the secret agony of my soul as I sunk into this companionship; compared these henceforth everyday associates with those of my happiest childhood – not to say with Steerforth, Traddles and the rest of those boys – and felt my hopes of growing up to be a learned and distinguished man, crushed in my bosom…*

…*From Monday morning until Saturday night, I had no advice, no counsel, no encouragement, no consolation, no assistance, no support of any kind, from anyone, that I can call to mind, as I hope to go to heaven!*'

Next, take the bustling, ever-changing street alongside Embankment tube, up to Charing Cross Station.

As a young reporter in the Houses of Parliament, Dickens was very familiar with this area, and produced a number of sketches in which he used material from life around here to try to sell to local journals. (The first he ever sold was actually *A Dinner at Poplar Walk*, and all aspiring writers will understand his joy when he tells how he opened the letter from the publisher to find that his article had been accepted. He was so 'over-the-moon' that he wandered around all alone for several hours, unable to talk to anyone). These sketches were gathered together and published under the title *Sketches by Boz*. They were a reasonable success: the publishers Chapman & Hall were among those who noticed that the young Charles wrote about scenes from daily life in the city – the same scenes as other people – it was just that Dickens' writing was better than that of others. Chapman & Hall tentatively offered the 24-year-old Dickens authorship of a new publication, based on the adventures of a certain Mr Pickwick, the consequences of which decision they could never possibly have begun to imagine.

Front cover of *Sketches by Boz* – George Cruickshank, 1837.

Why Boz? Charles' younger brother, Augustus, was called 'Moses' in the family which in turn came from the popular novel *The Vicar of Wakefield*. When playfully mispronounced through a blocked nose, this became 'Boses', which in turn became 'Boz'. The public was initially perplexed as can be seen from this verse in *Bentley's Miscellany* of March 1837:

> Who the dickens 'Boz' could be
> Puzzled many a learned elf,
> Till time unveiled the mystery,
> And 'Boz' appeared as Dickens' self.

One early story from 1837 set in this area is called *Early Coaches*. It is funny: typical Dickens in that it is a small incident, noted down and writ large. Dickens arrives at the, then, famous coaching inn opposite Charing Cross called 'Golden Cross' to board a coach. It has not arrived and so he prepares a refreshment of brandy and hot water, only to have the coach suddenly arrive, meaning he has to jump on leaving his eagerly anticipated drink to a very thankful and undeserving clerk.

You may also copy, in your imagination, a perplexed Mr Pickwick on the station forecourt, scurrying as best he can away from an irate cab driver who is convinced the innocent chap is an informer. This is because, in the interests of simply recording human behaviour on behalf of The Pickwick Club, he has been asking too many questions and writing down the answers in a notebook. Further comic kerfuffles ensue before Mr Pickwick and friends finally depart on the coach to Rochester and on to a great many more kerfuffles.

No expense is spared in the launch of the second series of *Sketches by Boz*, where, once again, George Cruikshank was asked to provide the artwork for the cover.

The station forecourt, scene of comic fisticuffs for Mr Pickwick.

We can imagine, too, between here and Covent Garden, a poor little waif – ten years old in the fictional account, *David Copperfield*; twelve years in reality – eeking out his weekly pay for food and treats. He tells us that he quickly became a connoisseur of pudding: a shop near St Martin's Church sold a very nice pudding, full of currants, but it was twice the price of a more bland but equally filling type – *'flabby'* with currants placed a long way apart – from another shop in the Strand. Down by the present Embankment tube was a *'miserable'* pub, *'the Lion, or the Lion and something'*, from which he could dine more expensively if he had the money. Here he might buy *'a saveloy and a penny loaf'* or a *'fourpenny plate of red beef'*. One very special time, he went to an *'alamode'* beef house in Drury Lane and asked for a *'small plate of beef'* which he ate with some bread he had brought with him. The waiter had rarely seen anything so comical as this young ragamuffin mixing with well dressed ladies and gentlemen, no doubt all out to see a show,

Opposite page: Would young David have dared to enter this fine restaurant in today's Drury Lane?

A view of Charing Cross, the station and hotel today, viewed from the Tube entrance across the road.

and he called his colleague over to watch. We can only imagine the burning shame of the little chap who was out on his own because his father was imprisoned for debt and who had had to earn his meager supper money rubbing shoulders with Mealy Potatoes. *'I am a gentleman, yes I am, really…'*.

Charles Dickens/David Copperfield drank ale with meals in the morning and at other times as water was often dangerous. On one special occasion, maybe he thinks his birthday, he went into a pub and asked for a glass of 'very best' ale. The landlady gave it to him, though probably somewhat diluted, bending down to give him a kiss and his money back at the same time.

The Adelphi Theatre is just up the road. Young David remembers wandering around here as it had tantalizing alleys and passageways. Later in life, Dickens would cooperate with

Above: The view down Villiers Street. The Embankment Tube sign can be seen – this was the location of the Blacking Factory. Also, somewhere in the same vicinity was the *'miserable'* pub, *'the Lion or the Lion and something'*.

Right: St Martin in the Fields church, just across the road from Charing Cross. Dickens gave a fund-raising talk here for the benefit of Great Ormond Street Children's Hospital. It started with 10 beds and is now the foremost authority in children's healthcare in the world.

Opposite page: A modern view of the bustling Strand with the Adelphi Theatre on the left hand side of the road.

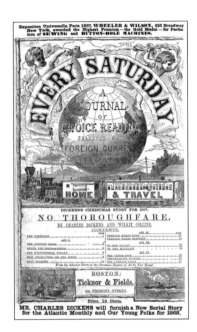

No Thoroughfare appears in The Christmas 1867 edition of the American journal *Every Saturday.*

Dickens in a portrait by Francis Alexander. It is 1842 and the thirty-year-old author is working on *Martin Chuzzlewit.* Very soon *A Christmas Carol* will sweep all before it, defining Christmas for most people right up to the present day.

his good friend, Wilkie Collins, to adapt the Christmas story *No Thoroughfare* and put it on at this theatre. It was an enormous success and ran for over 150 performances. It made a fortune. Did it make Dickens content? Silly question.

Also, at the time, this area was a good place to find lodgings. In *David Copperfield* Mrs Crupp gave David, his Aunt and Mr Dick an apartment here following Betsey Trotwood's financial 'ruin' by unscrupulous persons who would soon be most satisfyingly undone by the lion-hearted, if occasionally shambolic, Mr Micawber. Aunt Betsey soon brings the landlady to heel by hilariously demonstrating who is in charge of the flat and her beloved 'Trotwood'. She *'struck such terror to the breast of Mrs Crupp, that she subsided into her own kitchen, under the impression that my aunt was mad.'*

There is a happy scene towards the finale of *Martin Chuzzlewit*, at the other end of the Strand, near Fleet Street. The novel is largely about selfishness and how each main character loses it – apart from the tragic-comic hypocrite, Pecksniff, and the incorrigible and evil Jonas Chuzzlewit. Martin returns from America, near-death and a changed man, and relishes the opportunity to be of service to his manservant/ friend, Mark Tapley when they find themselves without accommodation in the Strand. He secures *'two garrets for himself and Mark, situated in a court in the Strand not far from Temple Bar'*. He has their luggage transferred there, *'and it was with a glow of satisfaction, which as a selfish man he never could have known and never had, that, thinking how much pains and trouble he had saved Mark, and how pleased and astonished Mark would be, he afterwards walked up and down, in the Temple, eating a meat pie for his dinner.'*

Temple Bar, where Martin ate his meat pie.

5
Wellington Street to Covent Garden and Seven Dials

The Offices of Household Words *and* All the Year Round. *Drury Lane. Covent Garden – flowers for Dora and a red-faced man takes a large meat pudding out of a hat. Seven Dials: depressed dogs and anatomical fowls.*

THIS STROLL CAN CARRY on from that in the previous chapter, or it is full of interest on its own. It starts where the Strand meets Aldwych and heads up Wellington Street.

On the right, a short way up, is number 26, with a café underneath. This is one of the most important addresses in literary London as it is where Dickens supervised his hugely successful weekly magazines *Household Words* (1850-59) and *All the Year Round* (1859-70). Charles Dickens Jnr continued the latter successfully until 1893.

The Charles Dickens' Café with the offices of *Household Words* and *All the Year Round* upstairs.

Dickens, world-famous and bursting with energy at the age of 38, decided to launch *Household Words* as a general magazine to show that, in all things, *'there is Romance enough, if we will find it out'*. Priced at only tuppence it came out every Wednesday beginning on 27 March 1850. Immediately, along with fiction and general pieces, it championed social reform and contributed to the reforms in the sewerage system following the 'Great Stink', mentioned earlier. Dickens serialized *Hard Times* and *A Child's History of England* in it too, and he attracted some eminent writers, Sir Edward Bulwer-Lytton, John Forster and Wilkie Collins among them, to contribute to it. The most eminent female author of the day, George Eliot, declined as she was not too keen on the idea of weekly serialization.

A row, culminating (with great irony considering Dickens' unrelenting attacks on the legal system in *Bleak House* a few years earlier, in the Court of Chancery), led to the closure of the magazine in 1859. Dickens had separated from his wife of over

Above left: Charles Dickens Jnr.

Above centre: Young Catherine Hogarth – a portrait in oils by Daniel Maclise.

Above right: Mrs Dickens in middle age. She wrote a cookbook in her leisure time.

twenty years, Catherine, in May 1858, and this was potentially a much bigger scandal than we can imagine today. The 'celebrity press' such as it was – its language was righteous rather than shrill – speculated on the possibility of adultery. Dickens was appalled but was also savvy enough to know that this unwelcome attention might affect his popularity and, bottom line perhaps, his sales. When the publishers, Bradbury & Evans, refused to issue a defence of him in *Punch*, things got out of hand and *Household Words* was closed.

Glad to relate, it came back immediately in slightly different form as *All the Year Round*. This was more fiction-based and enjoyed even greater success. Weekly sales could average 100 000 – two or three times the previous endeavour – and peaking at Christmas on 300 000.

Notable highlights included serialization of *A Tale of Two Cities*, *Great Expectations* and, from Wilkie Collins, one of my all-time favourites, *The Woman in White*, as marvellous a

The perfect spot, just adjacent to this walk, where you may find some fine old books.

page-turner as there ever was. It also printed *The Moonstone* by the same author which contains the wonderful quote and piece of advice: '*We had our breakfasts – whatever happens in a house, robbery or murder, it doesn't matter, you must have your breakfast.*' Dickens' collaborative work with Collins, *No Thoroughfare*, which, as discussed in the last chapter, went on to make a fortune just down the road at the Adelphi Theatre, also appeared here first.

Following Dickens' death his son, Charles who, business-wise up to this time had not seemed destined to 'git past Tuesday', as we say in Norfolk, took it over and ran it profitably until 1893.

If you are very, very lucky, you can sometimes find a copy of one above weekly magazines in secondhand bookshops shops or charity shops, maybe even in the nearby bookshops of Charing Cross Road, an excursion that makes a fabulous day out but a little beyond our 'brief' here.

Dickens at the time of writing a *Tale of Two Cities* and *Great Expectations*. The portrait of the author seated, with his left hand in his pocket, is by William Powell Frith.

Drury Lane Theatre today.

Turning right past the offices leads you to Drury Lane, which runs parallel to Wellington Street. It is here, in the pages of *The Old Curiosity Shop*, that we find the lodgings of the comical Mr Richard Swiveller. Mr Swiveller had seen an advertisement in the tobacconist above which shop he lived. Now, it so happens that the card in the window had referred to *'apartments'* , that is, plural, *'for a bachelor gentleman'*. In Dickens' words: ' *...Mr Swiveller, following up the hint, never failed to speak of it as his rooms, his lodgings, or his chambers, conveying to his hearers a notion of indefinite space, and leaving their imaginations to wander through long suites of lofty halls.'*

Here also is Drury Lane Theatre, the oldest theatre in England, dating back to 1663 when it was patronized by Samuel Pepys and sometimes favoured, two centuries later, by Dickens and the staff at Wellington Street if they had a special occasion to celebrate, which must have been pretty often. It has quite a handful of friendly ghosts, including a Man in

Grey, who can apparently be very helpful in encouraging and guiding nervous actors about the stage. It was not at this time doing very well, Shakespeare proving a particular disaster in financial terms. It must have occurred to Dickens' fine business mind to write a stage production for the stage here.

Coming back 'around the block' again to Wellington Street, take a left along Russell Street. This will bring you to Covent Garden. Dickens was known to take rooms in the Piazza here sometimes when his houses were not available for whatever reason. Tom and Ruth in *Martin Chuzzlewit* wander here early in summer mornings. They had both had a terrible time – Tom unjustly sacked by the pernicious hypocrite, Pecksniff, and Ruth humiliated as governess to what we might today call an uneducated and very rude 'nouveau riche' family with ideas way above their station. As a harbinger of vastly improved fortune for both of them just around the corner they have these lovely early morning strolls as regular as clockwork '*snuffing up*' – what fantastic English! – the perfume of the fruits and flowers, pineapples and melons, veal (stuffed but yet uncooked), '*lusty snails and fine young curly leeches.*'

David Copperfield buys flowers for Dora in the market here. I am reminded of two elderly sisters who told me whilst researching a previous book (*When Schooldays were Fun*, Halsgrove 2010) how they would get up really early on Spring mornings in their country village and pick primroses. These would have to be ready for the early-morning train to Covent Garden. They received 1p a bunch for them. This would have been in the 1920s, but it is a charming story and it is nice to think that, mixing fact and fiction, David might well have bought flowers picked by these ladies' forebears.

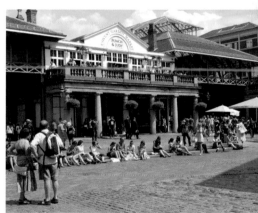

Above and opposite page:
Covent Garden, where Dickens would sometimes rent rooms and where he had his encounter with the man with the large meat pie in his hat.

Dickens tells us of a most bizarre scene he witnessed on one of his famous night walks. He had been walking all night, the sun was about to make an appearance and he sought a hot drink in a café in Covent Garden. In came a man in a snuff-coloured coat, shoes and a hat – nothing else as he could make out. This man had a very red face shaped like a horse. He ordered a pint of tea, a small loaf, a plate and a knife. Then, out of his hat he produced a very large cold meat pudding. This was placed on the plate and he proceeded to stab it, overhand, with the knife which was wiped on his sleeve. He then tore the pie apart with his hands and ate it all up. Dickens witnessed this happen twice. On the second occasion, the man asked the café-owner if he (the man with the hat) had a particularly red face. The owner replied, yes, indeed, his face was very red that morning. The man then confided that his mother had liked her drink and that he had stared at her hard in her coffin and the redness had transferred to him. Thereafter Dickens could not bring himself to go into the café again.

Heading north through any of the streets will bring you to Long Acre. If you cut through northwards again, maybe up Mercer Street, you will come to what is now an extremely – as Dickens might say – '*à la mode*' area of chocolatiers, coffee shops and expensive knick-knack establishments, known as Seven Dials.

In Dickens' day, this and the adjacent area of St Giles was dreadful as regards poverty and disease. He refers to it in his *American Notes* where he compares an area of New York, known as the Five Points, to it in terms of '*filth and wretchedness*'. This kind of writing brought him great, but luckily fairly quickly forgiven, animosity from citizens of the erstwhile colony. It is surprising to me that he does not use this part of London more in his great works, but I guess such areas also existed down by the Thames and he loved nothing more than placing his characters by the water.

A fine view across the roofs of London from Covent Garden towards the river: the London Eye can just be seen. Dickens liked to get up to the rooftops and describe the view, as he did when writing of Mrs Todger's boarding house; and Scrooge spends a fair amount of time flying over the grimy city.

54

The Seven Dials Monument today. Each dial, facing a slightly different direction, is crafted to give the time, when the sun is out, no matter to which dial you refer.

Dickens went down a storm in America, apart from when he criticized the erstwhile colony. In *Martin Chuzzlewit*, Martin and Mark are swindled whilst trying to buy land there, and almost die. He was quickly forgiven his criticisms however. Here, he is portrayed as a very flamboyantly dressed British lion in America.

This page and opposite: No 'depressed dogs and anatomical fowls' today – this area is a bustling, fashionable shopping/eating/drinking venue. Lots of people treat it like a smaller Piccadilly Circus, sitting all over, and not realizing that cars drive around the dial, having to sometimes shift pretty quickly.

Once, though, when he was just 23 and still struggling, he wrote a piece for *Bell's Life* magazine. He records the impressions of a traveller, new to the streets here. He talks of half-naked children wallowing in 'kennels'; of bird fanciers (and he is sure that if any bird is allowed out of the neighbourhood it will never come back), and broker's shops which would appear to have been established as homes for destitute bugs. He ends, in a warning of what is about to come for his readers, with a blistering and typically Dickensian adjective-strewn tirade. He sees *"dirty men, filthy women, squalid children, fluttering shuttlecocks, noisy battledores, reeking pies, bad fruit, more than doubtful oysters, attenuated cats, depressed dogs, and anatomical fowls…"*

Monmouth Street leads directly from Seven Dials to West End Theatreland.

6

Holborn Tube, Kingsway, Lincoln's Inn Fields, Temple Bar and up Chancery Lane to Grays Inn

The Law is an Ass, but an Ass can be made to sprint a bit. Mouldy Banks. Spontaneous combustion.

Lincoln's Inn is today quite grand with lovely houses and a park much loved by office workers when the sun shines.

THIS IS A WALK, roughly square, beginning at Holborn Tube Station. The London tube was begun in 1863, only seven years before Dickens' death, and it was left to later writers, notably Sir Arthur Conan Doyle, to utilize its dramatic potential in their stories. It was quick, efficient and cheap and either Holborn or Chancery Lane Tube, just a bit farther up the road, would have enabled a fast getaway from this part of town.

This, one feels, would have pleased Dickens as this was the setting for the interminable processes of the law. You never got away from here, at least metaphorically speaking. This was where perfectly good-natured souls became ground down in legal concrete, lost all

their money, became deranged and died. This was the kingdom of Jarndyce v. Jarndyce.

Head down Kingsway from Holborn Tube and take the first left into Lincoln's Inn Fields. Dickens was at his best when angry and the labyrinthine procedures of the law were one thing that made him very angry, indeed. Not that the rulers of the kingdom always minded: Sir Leicester Dedlock, one of the parties to the Jarndyce suit in *Bleak House*, could find nothing really wrong with an interminable Chancery suit. Indeed, being *'a slow, expensive, British constitutional kind of thing,'* it was quite comforting, even if it did involve *'an occasional delay of justice and a trifling amount of confusion'*. The process had been designed by his forefathers as a summit of human wisdom and any attacks on it by the lower classes would inevitably encourage revolution. So he was content to let it go on, being fleeced and deceived by his own solicitor, Tulkinghorn, all the while. Eventually he lost his wife too, the beautiful Lady Dedlock, who perished of despair and a broken heart on the grave of her former lover, Nemo, not far from where we are standing now.

Above left: The Ghost's Walk by Hablot Browne (Phiz). *Frankenstein*, by Mary Shelley, had been published when Dickens was six years old. It must have had a profound impact on him, as it does for all of us. There is an edge of terror to this portrayal of Bleak House which Dickens would, of course, have sanctioned.

Generally, bureaucracy was killing the nation. Two years previously, Dickens had written an essay, *A Poor Man's Tale of a Patent*. His Patent Office is based here, too. The poor chap trying to get a patent has to go to over a dozen offices, from here to Somerset House in the Strand, each time paying a fee to the total sum of ninety-six pounds, seven and eightpence. I wonder if the modern process is very much better? Would a modern entrepreneur agree with our hero that he was made to wonder if, in *'seeking an ingenious improvement meant to do good'*, he has actually done something wrong? *'All inventors taking out a Patent MUST feel so'*, he says. *'How else can a man feel, when he is met with such difficulties at every turn'*?

Dickens returns to the subject a few years later in *Little Dorrit*, with the fabulously named Circumlocution

Above right: Hablot Browne (Phiz) designed this cover for *Little Dorrit* in 1855.

A warning sign today: many were the unfortunate Victorian citizens driven to drink and despair by the interminable proceedings of the legal system in this part of town.

Office. This is a Kafkaesque place of eternal confusion, where you need a piece of paper in order to look at another piece of paper. And another, and another.

At the bottom of Kingsway you meet The Aldwych and turning left and left again at the Strand, you come to Temple Bar. Here we come across another Dickens' bête noire – banks, and, in particular, Tellson's Bank as depicted in *A Tale of Two Cities*. This bank is a *'triumphant perfection of inconvenience'*. Those of us who have been pursued by present day banks over our £200 overdraft whilst the bank itself manages to chalk up literally tens of billions of yearly losses - the staff being charged with talking to us of 'prudence' – may justifiably smile grimly here at Dickens' words. He goes a bit far, I think, with imagery of cesspools, decomposition, and *'insensate brutality'* but, yes, it resonates with us too, over 150 years later. We must remember all the time that his own father was imprisoned for debt and the misery this caused the 12 year old boy. Mr Micawber, who cannot manage his finances, is also always marginally the hero, while his sunny aspect ensures his eventual triumph as an emigrant in Australia.

The funniest bit, I think, is when Dickens has expurgated his soul, and calms down: *'When they took a young man into Tellson's London House, they hid him somewhere till he was old. They kept him in a dark place, like a cheese, until he had the full Tellson flavour and blue-mould upon him. Then only was he permitted to be seen…'*

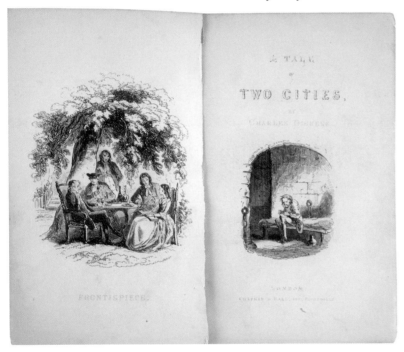

Hablot Knight Browne, known as Phiz, created the illustrations for *A Tale of Two Cities*. This is the title page from the first edition.

There is a good side to this area too. Holborn was, in the 1860s, a prime shopping area. In *My Father as I Recall Him*, Mamie Dickens talks of visiting a shop at Christmas-time and spending a hour or more selecting toys. We don't know exactly where the shop was. Charles Dickens was bonhomie itself as he loved Christmas. Also this road passes beyond the accommodation of Fagin and Nancy, to the stamping ground of Scrooge in my personal favourite, *A Christmas Carol*.

In this area, too, Dickens lets Tom Pinch and his sister walk in *Martin Chuzzlewit*. This was a *'good thing'* . Ruth was maybe another symbol of his idealized version of womanhood. As she walked, *'the Temple fountain might have leaped up twenty feet to greet the spring of hopeful maidenhood…'*. There is no justification for such an assessment. She is a nice young lady, but has up to this point shown no heroism or an awful lot of character. Dickens could present men, such as David Copperfield or his esteemed 'black angel', Steerforth, in quite complex ways but does not seem to have the same success with his female characters, who all too often appear to exist just to get happily married, as Ruth does, at the end of the book.

'Garden-court, down by the river' cannot be found now. You can feel the atmosphere, though. Wander down from Temple towards the great river. Imagine young Pip, confused as to who has given him his allowance – surely it is Miss Havisham and he will shortly be in the arms of Estella when he has finally learned how to become a gentleman – closing his book in his lodgings at St Paul's, ready for bed. All the clocks around strike eleven. He hears a sound. There is someone there! Who can be outside his window at this time of night?

It is a strange man; Magwitch. Pip learns that he, and not Miss Havisham, is responsible for his allowance. Magwitch has never forgotten Pip's kindness on the marshes at the very beginning of *Great Expectations*. Pip, however, feels humiliated and embarrassed at the revelation. The story is exciting but not perhaps very happy from now on. The book has

Nowadays the architecture in this part of town today has a swagger to it.

The Royal Courts of Justice.

two endings: one with no hope for Pip and Estella, and the other with some hope, at least as far as friendship is concerned. No hope or half hope – I prefer the latter.

Retrace your steps now until you see the Royal Courts of Justice ahead of you. Turn right and then left into Chancery Lane. First or second left will take you into Lincoln's Inn Fields. We began this chapter there with Sir Leicester Dedlock and it feels right to end it there too, as this was the scene of one of the most controversial episodes in Dickens – the fate of Krook.

Before this, however, let us just mention two other notable local 'firms' in *Bleak House*. Firstly, in Cook's Court, Cursitor Street, we find the Law Stationer, Mr Snagsby. Many would say that it is typical of Dickens that Mr Snagsby is *'a mild, bald, timid man, with a shining head'*, who is totally dominated by Mrs Snagsby. *'Rumour, always flying, bat-like, about Cook's Court and skimming in and out of everyone's windows, does say that Mrs Snagsby is jealous and inquisitive; and that Mr Snagsby is sometimes worried out of house and home, and that if he had the spirit of a mouse he wouldn't stand it.'*

Krook's shop might have been down an alley like this...

The other significant firm, in Lincoln Inn Fields itself, is that of Mr Tulkinghorn, solicitor to Sir Leicester Dedlock. He lives in a grand house – probably actually modelled on that of Dickens' lifelong friend, John Forster – much of which is let out to the legal profession and, in consequence, in this house *'lawyers lie like maggots in nuts'*. In a key scene from *Bleak House*, Mr Tulkinghorn visits Snagsby with terrible consequences for all.

The fate of Krook, however, who lives with his cat in his rag and bone, bric a brac and goodness-knows-what-else shop just here was to cause great debate on publication. Had Dickens lost it this time? Krook dies of spontaneous combustion. Mr Guppy and Tony have the misfortune to discover his charred remains. Some contemporaries thought that this was unworthy of the novelist – sensationalism for its own sake.

This is a subject that fascinated Dickens – like Mesmerism – and he refers to spontaneous combustion also in *Sketches by Boz*, *Martin Chuzzlewit* and *A Christmas Carol*. Dickens presents it as a consequence of evil – *'inborn, inbred, engendered in the corrupted humours of the viscious body itself'*.

7

A zig-zag walk from St Paul's to Monument Tube, Mansion House and up to Smithfield

Todgers'. The perils of gravy. Smithfield. Bah, humbug! The law is a bit sozzled.

SIR CHRISTOPHER WREN'S St Paul's Cathedral, finished in 1711, is the backdrop to many of Dickens' scenes. It signifies, generally, hope in the face of adversity and could be seen from virtually all over London. Today it must share the skyline with modern structures bearing such names as 'The Gherkin' and 'The Shard of Glass'.

When wandering down from the Cathedral towards the river today, the old sometimes seems almost literally squeezed out by the new.

St Paul's Cathedral today from the south east. David takes Peggotty to the top in *David Copperfield*.

The Monument, clean and bright as it is today.

This shot of The Monument with people gathered around it gives an idea of the immensity of the structure. It cost almost £13 500 to build and remains the tallest isolated stone pillar in the world.

Just along the river bank, a little inland, lies The Monument. In *Martin Chuzzlewit*, which Dickens himself thought his finest work (although extremely disappointing sales showed that the general public disagreed), we have an amazing description of the area of London around The Monument. This is where Todgers' accommodation for young gentlemen was found:

'You couldn't walk about Todgers' neighbourhood, as you could in any other neighbourhood. You groped your way for an hour through lanes and bye-ways, and courtyards, and passages; and you never once emerged upon anything that may reasonably be called a street. A kind of resigned distraction came over the stranger as he trod those devious mazes, and, giving himself up for lost, went in and out and round about and quietly turned back again when he came to a dead wall, or was stopped by an iron railing, and felt that the means of escape might possibly present themselves in their own good time, but that to anticipate them was hopeless.'

You fell over pubs:

'To tell of half the queer old taverns that had a drowsy existence near Todgers', would fill a goodly book; while a second volume no less capacious might be devoted to an account of the quaint old guests who frequented their dimly lighted parlours.'

Everywhere there was wiggledyness and confusion; smoke and noise. This is the view from the roof of Todgers' itself:

The area around The Monument is bright and busy today after almost five million pounds was spent on renovations. No longer Dickens' 'wilderness upon wilderness...'.

65

The Monument from Fish Hill Street. It was erected originally to signify where the Great Fire of London started, which in reality was actually about fifty yards away in Pudding Lane. As the name suggests, this was an area of bakers' shops and the story goes that one person failed to put out his oven fire before going to bed. The houses were made of wood and the conflagration was immense, burning for three days.

'There were steeples, towers, belfries, shining vanes, and masts of ships: a very forest. Gables, housetops, garret-windows, wilderness upon wilderness. Smoke and noise enough for all the world at once.'

The year is 1843 and Dickens is to very much concentrate his energies on this area, first in *Martin Chuzzlewit* (though poor sales led to the incongruous plot idea of whipping Martin and Mark Tapley off to near death in America before returning, less selfish, broke and redeemed, to England for happy endings), and then in my personal number one, *A Christmas Carol*, which was published in December of that year and went through six editions very smartly indeed.

Dickens was always much aware of making the reader hungry, or thirsty, and it seems to me that, during 1843, we have some of the best – and funniest – writing on the subject of food. Almost immediately upon meeting Mrs Todgers we learn of the anxiety and stress caused by providing enough gravy for her resident gentlemen. It has aged her twenty years she confides to the two Miss Pecksniffs. She continues, in what I believe to be the only anti-gravy tirade in English Literature: *'There is no such passion in human nature, as the passion for gravy among commercial gentlemen It's nothing to say a joint won't yield – a whole animal wouldn't yield – the amount of gravy they expect each day at dinner. And what I have undergone in consequence,' cried Mrs Todgers, raising her eyes and shaking her head, 'no-one would believe!'*

Later there is dinner – usually served at two but today at five to give extra time for cooking as there are special guests – served by the comical young Bailey, whom, according to Mrs Todgers, the young gentlemen spoil to the extent *'that I'm afraid nothing but hanging will ever do him any good'*. Dinner consists of boiled beef, roast veal, bacon, pies and *'an abundance of such vegetables as are favourably known to housekeepers for their satisfying qualities'*. All is washed down with bottles of stout, bottles of wine, bottles of ale, *'and divers other strong drinks, native and foreign.'*

And one assumes, lots of gravy.

Leaving Todgers and walking up King William Street, we come to Bank, Cornhill and Threadneedle Street. Between here and Mansion House existed the financial centre of the British Empire. This is where Scrooge and Mr Dombey would barter and bargain, and buy and sell debts, ruining countless souls in the process.

Martin Chuzzlewit and Mark Tapley in America. Having been swindled into buying a disease-ridden swamp in the belief that it was a prime building land, Martin almost dies and is cared for by Mark. Here we see him leaning on his friend as he gradually regains his strength. This illustration, by Solomon Eytinge Jnr, appeared in the 1867 American edition of *Martin Chuzzlewit*.

67

Above left: Bank Tube leads out into the financial centre.

Above right: The indignity of time, forever marching onward and upward! The venerable Royal Exchange begins to be overshadowed by the NatWest Building (left of picture) and the Swiss Re Building (right), affectionately known as the 'Gherkin', although one very young lady I know suggests a much better nickname would be 'Back-of-a-Bee-Upside-Down'.

A Christmas Carol is remarkable for many things, but one of the most striking is that while it deals in great themes – love, selfishness, redemption – it is the most vague of Dickens' great novels in describing exactly where we are at any one time. Of course, a lot of it is spent whisking Scrooge over the universe and from life to death to life again, with a touch of time-travel thrown in. But as to its earthly origins, most people know that it is based somewhere in the East End of London but will not be able to tell you more than that. However, at the beginning, as Dickens begins to warm to his theme of Christmas – cold, gaslight, 'gruff' old church bells, braziers, rapture of everyone for the time of year, holly, oranges, plums, nuts, stirring Christmas puddings in garrets, skating on the snow, singing carols, good cheer, meanness and forgiveness – he refers to *'The Lord Mayor, in the stronghold of the mighty Mansion House'* who is giving instructions to his fifty cooks and butlers to keep Christmas as a Lord Mayor should. So we know where Scrooge is when he utters the immortal words *'Bah, humbug!'*

When I was younger I was lucky enough to share a London house with several other people, all of whom were great Dickens fans. Every Christmas Eve, those of us who did not go somewhere else had a ritual that I cannot help but smile about whenever I think back. We would make sure that we had finished dinner and washed up etc. by about 8pm. Then, we would settle down in a circle on the living room carpet with coffee, mints, nuts, tawny port and Guinness. We would take it in turns to read the whole of *A Christmas Carol*

Marley's Ghost.

John Leech

Henry Charles Bryant, a contemporary of Dickens (although he lived much longer – he died just after the start of the First World War), created this work in oils which perfectly captures the world of Christmas treats to be had just outside Scrooge's window. Dickens loved to make his readers see, smell and taste all kinds of food. Mamie, his daughter, remarks on this and yet says that, in his private life, he was very frugal at mealtimes.

Scrooge, in his unreformed state as the world's greatest curmudgeon, 'enjoys' his Christmas Eve. He has had his gruel and sits by a sparse fire in semi-darkness. He liked darkness because it was cheap.

Dickens'
handwritten
title to
A Christmas Carol.

Right: Tiny Tim by Frederick
Barnard, published as
frontispiece to the 1870 edition
of *A Christmas Carol.*

Below: Scrooge greets his third
visitor in *A Christmas Carol.* By
John Leech, 1843.

aloud. We had a particularly gruff-sounding flatmate who would say Scrooge's lines with such brilliance that we would often have to stop for a few minutes, quite helpless with laughter. It was maybe fortunate that he had the invariable habit of nodding off about the same time as the second apparition occurred: this would be about 11 o'clock. The art, of course, was to make sure that the final words from Tiny Tim – *'God Bless Us, Everyone!'* – were said just after the clock struck twelve. In all the years we did it, I think we always achieved this (you can speed up or slow down, you see, or have another nut or something to keep on time…).

Mansion House is also the area we find Sam Weller sauntering about, thinking and scheming how to help his hapless but golden-hearted master, Mr Pickwick. Dickens, always the romantic, has him stop in front of a stationers's shop, where he espies a valentine's card. But can the mischievous 24-year-old author present this in a suitably soft-focused, loving fashion? Well, perhaps that was asking too much:

'The particular picture on which Sam Weller's eyes were fixed, as he said this, was a highly-coloured representation of a couple of human hearts skewered together with an arrow, cooking

The Royal Exchange was founded in 1565, the present building being opened by Queen Victoria in 1844, the year after the launch of *A Christmas Carol*. This probably did not inconvenience Scrooge too much as stockbrokers were banned as being extremely rude. Although not strictly a stockbroker himself, just a general tradesman in human debt and misery and *very, very* rude, it is hard to imagine Scrooge being allowed inside. We must picture him prowling about outside trying to buy and sell lists of debtors. No doubt, however, Ralph Nickleby was allowed in as he had an altogether more 'upper class' clientele.

Left: Today, the area flanked by The Royal Exchange – now an upmarket shopping centre – and the Bank of England is a favourite spot for city workers to eat their lunchtime sushi. The memorial is to the workers of the City who lost their lives in the First World War, while the statue commemorates the Duke of Wellington.

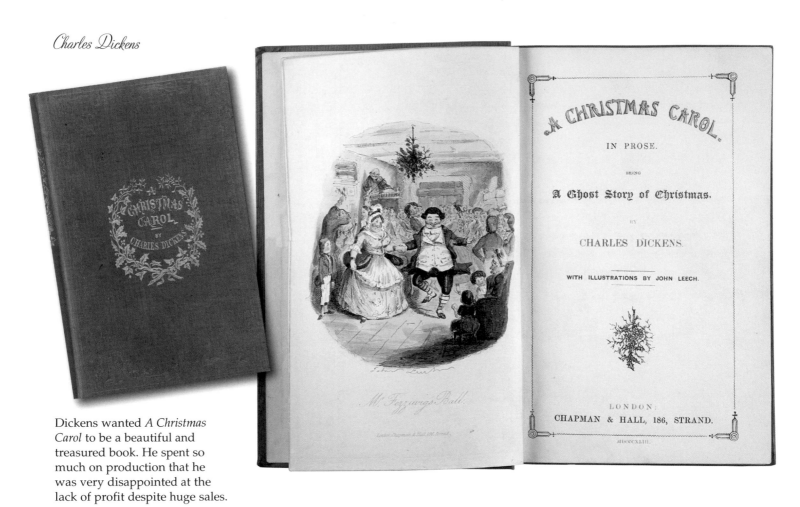

Dickens wanted *A Christmas Carol* to be a beautiful and treasured book. He spent so much on production that he was very disappointed at the lack of profit despite huge sales.

before a cheerful fire… A decidedly indelicate young gentleman, in a pair of wings and nothing else, was depicted as superintending the cooking…'.

If you stroll towards the river at this point, you will come to London Bridge. This is not the same bridge as Dickens knew as that was sold for almost two and a half million pounds in 1968 and shipped, stone by stone, to Arizona where it has become the second largest tourist attraction in the State. The bridge featured in the great novels is the 'Rennie Bridge' – named after the designer – and was opened in 1831. Dickens tells how he liked to sit here and watch the world go by. David Copperfield is inspired by the golden top of The Monument, visible from the centre. Barnaby Rudge crosses the bridge also, but, in all fairness it has to be said that, in that novel, a lot of people cross a lot of bridges anyhow.

The most famous meeting at – well, *under* in this case – London Bridge was, of course, the fateful one involving Nancy and Mr Brownlow in *Oliver Twist*. This resulted in the murder of Nancy by Sikes – Dickens' most popular public reading which invariably brought the house down – and the eventual rescue of young Oliver.

Coming just north of the river you will cross Lower Thames Street. This is a pretty busy thoroughfare today, but it is where Dickens places Kate Nickleby and her mother, in a miserable, cold and ghostly old house courtesy of their more-than-mean uncle, Ralph.

A little farther north is Smithfield. This is the location of Mr Jaggers' office in *Great Expectations*. Young Pip has to come here and, as Mr Jaggers is not available, he goes for a walk to pass the time. *'So I came into Smithfield; and the shameful place, being all asmear with filth and fat and blood and foam, seemed to stick to me. So I rubbed it off with all possible speed by turning into a street where I saw the great black dome of St Paul's…'* He carries on and is

'Oh, Scrooge, mend your ways or you will shortly end up here!' This is a John Leech engraving.

Lower Thames Street today.

73

Smithfield today – in past centuries, the place for hangings, torture, and markets of several sorts.

Looking towards the central arch in Smithfield market.

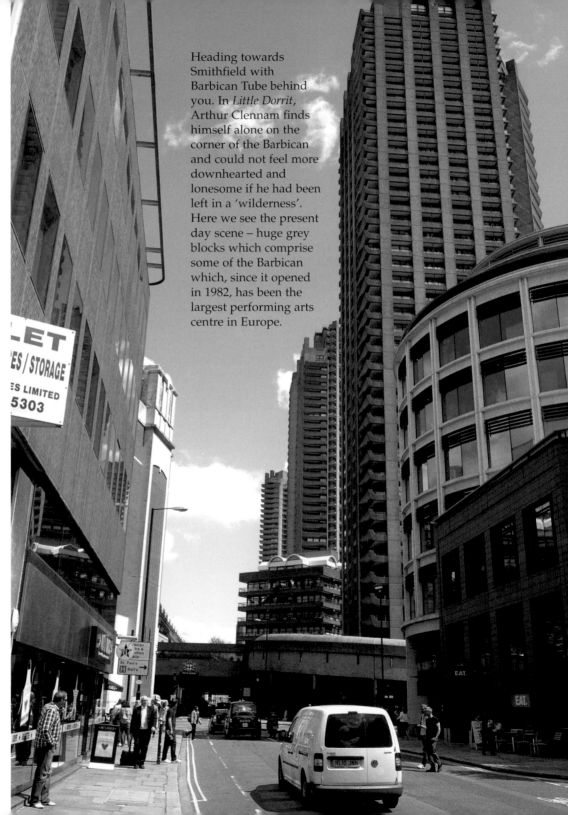

Heading towards Smithfield with Barbican Tube behind you. In *Little Dorrit*, Arthur Clennam finds himself alone on the corner of the Barbican and could not feel more downhearted and lonesome if he had been left in a 'wilderness'. Here we see the present day scene – huge grey blocks which comprise some of the Barbican which, since it opened in 1982, has been the largest performing arts centre in Europe.

confronted with a *'partially drunk'* minister of justice who tries to extort money from him by promising to show him the local gallows and the Debtors' Door out of which will come, at eight next morning, four convicted felons sentenced *'to be killed in a row'*. Pip is sickened and gives him a shilling to make him go away.

This area – City, Barbican, Smithfield, Barts Hospital and down to the Old Bailey – held a special place in Dickens' heart. Smithfield's gruesome appeal is easy to fathom. It had always been a place of blood, torture and death. William Wallace was strung behind a horse and dragged here in 1305 to be hanged, drawn and quartered. Much more hanging and torture followed. In Dickens' day, it was notorious as the scene of muggings, especially if you were not a local and your face did not 'fit'. Then, of course, until 1855, cattle were slaughtered here, as young Pip, above, found out. In *Oliver Twist*, Oliver and Sikes pass through here on the way to rob the Maylie house and we are told that *'the ground was covered, nearly ankle deep, with filth and mire'*. Smithfield is also mentioned in *Barnaby Rudge* and *Nicholas Nickleby*.

Some of the fine pubs in the area bear names associated with the meat trade.

A central eating area for the present city worker – pubs, sushi bars, delicatessens, greasy spoons and modern Italian cafés.

The original intricate metal gates are today picked out in vibrant colours.

So great was the noise and hubbub that, in an early piece entitled '*A Parliamentary Sketch*', Dickens compares Smithfield to the Houses of Parliament in session – not very complimentary to the latter august institution, one feels.

It is unrecorded what Dickens thought of the market in unwanted wives – brought here to be sold alongside cattle and bric a brac – that existed in the early 19th century.

A few hundred yards from Smithfield is St Bart's Hospital, London's oldest, founded in 1123. The immortal Mrs Gamp from *Martin Chuzzlewit* has a friend who works as a nurse here – Betsy Prig. Pip would no doubt have seen it on the way to Mr Jaggers' office in *Great Expectations*. A typical example of Dickens' eye for humorous detail comes in *Little Dorrit*. Arthur Clennam has recovered from his downhearted reverie as he stood in a corner of the Barbican, recounted above, and has helped escort an injured man into St Barts. The man has been hit by a coach. Arthur addresses the surgeon:

Alongside the road running through the current market are four of the most pristine telephone boxes imagineable – everywhere you go there is colour.

Barts Hospital entrance.

The Old Bailey. It was built on the site of the infamous Newgate Prison. People were hanged outside having first been taken from the gaol along Dead Man's Walk, until the practice was stopped in the 19th century, It is where Charles Darnay is put on trial for treason in *A Tale of Two Cities*.

Dickens, who loved exercise and thought nothing of walking 23 miles along the Kent coast at one stretch, or walking all night in London, would, I think, most enthusiastically approve of the bike racks outside St Barts. You can hire one and leave it in another bike rack elsewhere in the city. In fact, if your legs tire a little, you could use one for the routes in this book!

'It's a serious injury, I suppose?' said Clennam.

'Ye-es', replied the surgeon, with the thoughtful pleasure of an artist contemplating the work on an easel…'

From St Barts, you can look down the road and see the Old Bailey. As a young reporter in *Sketches by Boz*, Dickens says that he finds the system of justice dispensed here efficient but without heart. It is a subject he takes up with passion many times in his later career.

8

A walk around the West End of town, particularly looking at places where literary characters lived – or wish they did in the case of Mr Micawber – and worked

A debauched aristocrat. Nickleby territory. The Master of Deportment. A one-legged man.
Hanging highwaymen at Tyburn. Albertopolis. Mr Dombey sits alone.

Entering Leicester Square.

Leicester Square Tube.

THIS IS QUITE A HEFTY walk and could well take all day, depending how long you stop to wonder as you wander. Dickens spent a great deal of time 'up East', but there is no doubt he loved this part of the city equally and some of his greatest villains and cold hearts, such as Ralph Nickleby and Mr Dombey, lived here, as well as a number of his finest comic creations like Mr Turveydrop.

Starting at Green Park Tube, turn towards Piccadilly Circus and past The Ritz and Fortnum & Mason. This is Piccadilly, named after a maker of piccadillies – collars – in the 17th century. The area was not quite so grand in the 19th century as it is now, but very respectable: it was Mr Micawber's dream, when things improved financially, to live above a shop here. As it was, of course, he ended up an important man, but in Australia.

Chapman & Hall, Dickens' first publishers, were located at 193 Piccadilly from 1850.

Carry straight on to Leicester Square which is the location of Mr George's shooting gallery in *Bleak House*. Turning left at Charing Cross and left again along Shaftesbury Avenue will bring you to Piccadilly Circus.

From here, Regent Street sweeps northwards in an stately arc and it is where Dickens housed Lord Verisopht in *Nicholas Nickleby*. For some reason, although we don't know for sure, I have always imagined the *'handsome suite of private apartments'* to be in the first half of the street on the left hand side before reaching Hamleys. It is here, in *Nicholas Nickleby*, that we first meet this dissolute gentleman, at three o'clock in the afternoon, reclining listlessly on a sofa, his slippered foot dangling to the ground. He is yawning and comparing notes about the previous night's debauch with his constant companion, Sir Mulberry Hawk. They are bent on the dishonour of Miss Kate Nickleby (they are

Although Dickens is not specific, I have always imagined Lord Verisopht to have lived in this section of Regent's Street – the most elegant part of London's most elegant street.

Then, as now, Park Lane was the playground of the rich – this is the probable spot of the confrontation in a drinking establishment between Nicholas Nickleby and Lord Verisopht's entourage.

eventually undone by a sequence of events sparked off by a confrontation with Kate's brother, Nicholas, in an inn probably situated in Park Lane, just off Marble Arch and not far from here).

This is Nickleby country as far as London is concerned. Just off a side road to the right – try Beak Street – is Golden Square, home of Ralph Nickleby, uncle to Nicholas and, along with Squeers, chief villain of the piece. It is interesting to compare its opulence today to the atmosphere of the square in the mid 19th century as described in the novel:

'Although a few members of the graver professions live about Golden Square, it is not exactly in anybody's way to or from anywhere. It is one of the squares that have been; a quarter of the town that has gone down in the world, and taken to letting lodgings. Many of its first and second floors are let, furnished, to single gentlemen; and it takes boarders besides. It is a great resort of foreigners'.

Mr Ralph Nickleby sits in his dismal house dressed, as we meet him, as if to go out. He

Golden Square today.

theatres around here, although Ada was very uncomfortable at continually being pursued by the smitten Mr Guppy, and she was afraid that he would bankrupt himself by following her to every dramatic production.

A little past the 'Circus' on the right is Holles Street which leads to a very important Dickens location, Cavendish Square.

The junction of Oxford Street and Regent Street. Mr Turveydrop's Dancing Academy is a few minutes away (at the far end of Oxford Street) and Richard and Ada had lodgings here in *Bleak House*.

Lord George lives near here *in Barnaby Rudge* and, tellingly, having addressed his supporters (far too briefly – *'Gentlemen, No Popery. Good Day. God Bless you'* - which made them very discontented), they disperse to the adjoining fields. *'Here, they presently fell to pitch and toss, chuck-farthing, odd or even, dog fighting, and other Protestant recreations'*.

Mrs Mantolini's dress-making establishment could well have been in one of these handsome houses bordering the bright park in the middle of Cavendish Square.

By Marble Arch, tourists rush past the site of Tyburn, many of them probably unaware of the history of the spot. Tyburn gallows were a uniquely triangular affair, supported on three legs, which enabled up to 24 people to be hanged simultaneously. Oliver Cromwell was also hanged here although he was already dead: Charles II had him taken from his grave as a final act of humiliation.

The Albert Memorial on a beautiful sunny morning.

Inset: A close up of a gilded Prince Albert, sitting in almost religious pomp, surrounded by – some unworthy folk say actually 'sitting on' – the greatest thinkers of all time.

Although Dickens professed a wish to find an 'inaccessible cave' in order to escape from memorials to the Prince, the two men undoubtedly hold a strong connection. Both men worked hard and effectively for improvements to education, welfare and work in the booming factories at this time – mid 19th century, the height of Empire – and after Albert's untimely death in 1861 (most probably modern doctors believe, of cancer and hard work, the latter once again another connection with Dickens), the great novelist became more than ever the people's champion. The Queen was a great admirer, and had a private audience with Dickens shortly before his death.

Once back from your excursion to 'Albertopolis', walk a few yards down Oxford Street and turn first left. Immediately to the north is Marylebone and right in the middle is

The Royal Albert Hall. There is a further monument to him on the far side which is the site of the main entrance: this lies in, suitably, Prince Consort Road which leads directly into Princes Gardens.

Bryanston Square today.

BRYANSTON SQUARE W1
CITY OF WESTMINSTER

Bryanston Square. It is about ten or twelve minutes walk straight up Great Cumberland Street. Near here we find the home of Mr Dombey. He is particularly interesting in that he is not an out-and-out villain but more cold and deluded, unable to love his adoring daughter, after the very early demise of his son, Paul, who meant everything to him. (Paul's death, along with that of Little Nell, had the Victorian public in unprecedented grief and consternation).

Dickens allows Mr Dombey redemption at the end of the novel. However, the mood of gloom at the beginning of the novel is quickly established. When we enter Mr Dombey's house, in Chapter 3, it is described as being:

'on the shady side of a tall, dark, dreadfully genteel street in the region between Portland Place and Bryanston Square. It was a corner house, with great wide areas containing cellars frowned upon by barred window, and leered at by crooked-eyed doors leading to dustbins. It was a house of dismal state…'

What wonderful English is this! *'Dreadfully genteel…'*; *'a house of dismal state*?' Could anything be more suggestively gruesome?

It is not dissimilar to Ralph Nickleby's house just 'down the road'. Ralph, however, is allowed no redemption at the end of the novel as the amount of pain and death he has caused – including to Smike, his own son – is just too great. No, he must hang himself.

Edgware Road Tube is just up the road, or a 'bendy bus' or taxi will take you back to Green Park, where this walk began.

9
Yorkshire. Dotheboys Hall

Boys sent packing for good. A most peculiar curriculum. A letter from a fan.

YORKSHIRE IS FAMOUS in Dickens' work for one campaign primarily, but what a hammer blow it was! This is of course, his tilt at schools such as Wackford Squeers' Dotheboys Hall, and he is credited with the elimination of such evil establishments.

In 1823 there had been a famous case, Jones verses Shaw, which had shocked the nation. Young people were being sent to 'boarding schools' which advertised 'no holidays' which meant that, if you did not want the inconvenience of ever seeing your child, you could pay a fee to have them kept permanently away. And 'permanently' often meant just that, in a broader sense, as they could be subject to such malnutrition and abuse that their likely

Dotheboys Hall as it is today.

Greta Bridge, taken from the private garden of Lady Dorothy Gilbertson.

end would be in the local churchyard. Dickens went on a trip to Yorkshire to witness such schools for himself: he came across one in Bowes where the head was, unsurprisingly, resentful and uncommunicative. This head, on which Squeers was probably based, used to come down to the Saracen's Head Inn in Snow Hill, London, and invite guardians or parents to meet him there to arrange a fee for the complete removal of their inconvenient charges. He would then take them back to Yorkshire.

In *Nicholas Nickleby*, uncle Ralph comes across an advertisement:

'*EDUCATION – At Mr Wackford Squeers's Academy, Dotheboys Hall, at the delightful village of Dotheboys, near Greta Bridge in Yorkshire, Youth are boarded, clothed, booked, furnished with pocket money, provided with all necessaries, instructed in all languages living and dead, mathematics, orthography, geometry, astronomy, trigonometry, the use of the globes, algebra, single stick (if required), writing, arithmetic, fortification, and every other branch of classical literature. Terms, twenty guineas per annum. No extras, no vacations, and diet unparalleled. Mr Squeers is in town, and attends daily, from one till four, at the Saracen's Head, Snow Hill. NB An able assistant wanted. Annual salary 5 pounds. A Master of Arts would be preferred.*'

Young Nicholas, once recruited and having travelled up to Yorkshire, finds things somewhat different. It is his first lesson:

'"Please, sir, he's weeding the garden", replied a small voice. "To be sure," said Squeers, by no means disconcerted. "So he is. B-o-t, bot, t-i-n, tin, bottin, n-e-y, ney, bottiney, noun substantive, a knowledge of plants. When he has found that bottinney means a knowledge of plants, he goes out and knows 'em. That's our system, Nickleby: what do you think of it?"'

In *My Father as I Recall Him*, Mamie Dickens says that, since childhood, her father had possessed a quick perception of human character – the propensity for good and evil and many states besides. She makes the very interesting point that he valued his ability to present actual bits and pieces of human behaviour above and beyond any literary abilities he possessed. He would be far more pleased with a compliment regarding the former than the latter. His lifelong friend and first biographer, John Forster, noticed this as well. This is further emphasized in a book of 1895 – *Dickens: People and Places* – which is wonderfully placed to be able to quote from people still alive who knew him. He was apparently asked why many of his plots had the same characteristics, e.g., lots of things go wrong, then at the finish the protagonists come together, and everyone gets their due comeuppance, the most unworthy being required, usually, like Ralph Nickleby, to commit suicide? Why not make the ending a little more varied? He replied to the effect that he had neither the time nor patience. He was not over-concerned with literary merit or structure.

The same 1895 book, incidentally contains the wonderful statement: *'it may be said that the Dickens boom is now subsiding, having been somewhat overdone'*. Excuse me, but would you like to say that again?

Below left: Bowes churchyard: Mr Shaw, Headmaster of Dotheboys Hall, is buried here.

Below right: The George Hotel at Greta Bridge. The sign had been restored to the front of the (now) private residence a few days before this photograph was taken. A barbecue had been put on by the village as part of the celebrations for Dickens' 200th birthday.

Mamie Dickens also makes the point that her father's capacity for work was immense. I cannot believe it either – sometimes I think he breathes words as others breath air. Besides writing his great novels, he wrote thousands of letters. Unfortunately for us, he decided to have a great bonfire at Gad's Hill Place in 1860 when he burnt armful after armful of his correspondence. Why? We don't know and it is a literary tragedy. Mamie Dickens, though, gives us a tantalising glimpse of his style and his rapport with his young fans. He had received a letter about Squeers and he wrote back from Doughty Street, London, on 12 December 1838. Master Hastings Hughes had written to the great man making various suggestions about *Nicholas Nickleby*. The reply is lovely. Here is some of it:

'Respected Sir: I have given Squeers one cut on the neck, and two on the head, at which he appeared much surprised, and began to cry, which, being a cowardly thing, is just what I would have expected from him – wouldn't you?

I have carefully done what you told me in your letter about the lamb and the two 'sheeps' for the little boys. They have also had some good ale and porter and some wine. I am sorry you did not say what wine you would like them to have. I gave them some sherry, which they liked very much, except one boy who was a little sick and choked a good deal. He was rather greedy, and that's the truth, and I believe it went the wrong way, which I say served him right, and I hope you will say so too. Nick has had his roast lamb, as you said he was to, but he could not eat it all, and says if you do not mind his doing so he should like to have the rest hashed tomorrow with some greens, which he is very fond of, and so am I…

…Fanny Squeers shall be attended to, depend on it. Your drawing of her is very like, except that I do not think her hair is quite curly enough. The nose is particularly like hers, and so are the legs. She is a nasty, disagreeable thing, and I know it will make her very cross when she sees it, and what I say is that I hope it may…'

What a wonderful thing to receive as a young boy when you have had the temerity to write to the most famous author in the world! I dare say that the young lad dined off it for the rest of his life (I certainly would have!).

Original oil painting by Hablot Browne 'The Country Manager Rehearses a Combat: a scene from *Nicholas Nickleby*.'
(private collection)

10

Midlands and the North. Birmingham, Manchester and Preston. Hard Times. Lancashire. Warwickshire.

Kind employers. Victorian political correctness. A difficult read. Back to Doughty Street for a minute. Where did Little Nell wander? Mary Hogarth.

IN 1839, DICKENS set off on a tour of Manchester with Hablot Browne, possibly the finest illustrator of his books, and John Forster, his lifelong friend to whom he showed everything he wrote, and his first biographer. He had just completed *Oliver Twist*. His aim was to see the conditions in the cotton mills and, in particular, to support the Ten Hours Movement which sought to limit the number of hours that children could work. The full consequences of this tour were not to come about for some years when, in 1854, he published *Hard Times*. He famously sought to '*strike the heaviest blow in my power*' for the unfortunate young factory operatives.

Strangely, perhaps, the most immediate result was due to the fact that he met the Grant brothers, soon to gain immortality as the kindest bosses in the world: they became the Cheeryble Brothers in *Nicholas Nickleby*, his next novel. As he was often to do, he transferred their factory, lock stock and barrel elsewhere, on this occasion to somewhere off Threadneedle Street in London where they rescued the Nickleby family – he gave Nicholas a (strangely ill-defined) nice job, saw the family into an ideal house and everyone got married, to live happily ever after. The novel is a great one by any standards but in the almost unseemly haste with which happiness and virtue gain their just rewards over evil, we can almost imagine him saying, as mentioned above, '*I don't have the time, the inclination or the patience*' to do anything more complex.

Hard Times is reputed to take place in a cross between Manchester and Preston. The working lives of the mill operatives are indeed, appalling, but there is a more general theme as well.

Threadneedle Street. London – this area is probably where the Cheeryble Brothers had their business and where Nicholas Nickleby became happily employed.

In modern terms we could say that Dickens set out to expose the tragedy that is 'political correctness' gone berserk – in his time Utilitarianism. This was the belief in rationality and *'the greatest amount of happiness for the greatest number of people'*. Rational behaviour was to rule; children should be taught *'facts, facts, facts'*; imagination was to be curtailed; tall poppies were to be cut down; everyone should make widgets for they made *money*.

It is a fearful novel in many ways, very difficult to read for me. It is dry, dusty with hypocrisy (by the likes of bosses like Mr Josiah Bounderby) at every turn, with more than a hint of sexual exploitation: witness James Harthouse in his ultimately unsuccessful attempt to 'woo' Louisa after her arranged marriage to Josiah Bounderby who is thirty years her senior. Tom Gradgrind has an uncomfortably strong relationship with his sister and ends up a young drunk (oh, and he robs a bank, as well). So very often in his novels

Dickens lightens the mood of bad things by juxtaposing funny, warm and loving things. Here, he seems to give up. Still, some people whose opinion I respect, rate it his finest work. The eminent critic, F R Leavis, said it was the only novel of Dickens worthy of serious scrutiny, but I most respectfully disagree.

Hard Times was serialized in *Household Words* between 1 April and 12 August 1854. *North and South*, by Elizabeth Gaskell, a novel with distinct parallels, was published at about the same time. *Hard Times* sold very well: sales of the magazine held up at about 70 000 to 80 000 copies a month while the tale was told – this is staggering bearing in mind that many of his enthusiastic public could not read at all and had to pay someone to do it for them. Dickens was, reportedly *'three parts mad and the fourth part delirious'* with the public response. The reason is not hard to find, in my opinion. Never before had a great writer found the ordinary man and his feelings worthy of such scrutiny and, yes, affection. The downtrodden working man loved him back.

Dickens is a lot of fun north of London. Whereas in the south it is not always difficult to place his characters – he loved to go to Brighton or Dover and then across the Channel to France and Italy – he was not all that easy to trace when he ventured to the north of our country. A good many of his locations are generic – witness 'Coketown' above as a bit of Manchester and Preston (with some features of Birmingham!). Little has exercised his fans so much – including me – as to the exact wanderings of Little Nell in *The Old Curiosity Shop* when she decided to venture and lurch northwards, not south, before her untimely death. Of which, by the by, Thackeray said, in despair, that there was no competing with writing like this and reputedly chucked the manuscript out of the train window in which he was travelling. Oscar Wilde, on the other hand said *'You would have to have a heart of stone not to laugh'* at the death of Little Nell. At all events, it grabbed the attention of, not just England, but the world. It is reported that, when the latest monthly edition of the tale was about to be landed in New York, people lined the quay, yelling *'Is Little Nell dead? Is she dead?'* Publishing the novel in monthly parts, Dickens had left the world on a cliff-hanger – was she or wasn't she? As we all know now, she was.

No grief was greater than that of the author himself. Was it a partial lancing of the grief he had experienced in 48 Doughty Street, London, in the early years of his success when, after a visit to St James Theatre, 17 year old Mary Hogarth had inexplicably collapsed and died in his arms? Certainly, Dickens was very badly shaken when Little Nell left this literary life by his hand. Some critics think he had never recovered from the shock of Mary Hogarth's death. She was his sister-in-law and he utterly adored her. There followed the only time he missed a deadline as he could not work.

Little Nell and her Grandfather, an illustration by Fred Barnard, 1870s.

Charles Dickens

Doughty Street was, and is, a pleasant tree-lined street.

Charles and Catherine had their bedroom on the top floor, looking out into the street. Mary, his sister-in-law had the back bedroom, top floor. It was not unusual for an unwed sister to share the house of her married sibling.

One possible location for The Old Curiosity Shop, although some experts think it may have been nearer to Tottenham Court Road.

Endell Street today – possible route north for Little Nell in *The Old Curiosity Shop*.

Centre Point today marks the location of Tottenham Court Road and can be seen for miles. Did Little Nell pass this way? David Copperfield certainly did on his way to see Steerforth in the nearby British Musuem.

The splendid Major Bagstock and Mr Dombey meet the ladies, by Hablot Knight Browne (Phiz).

Her gravestone bears the legend: ' *Young, beautiful and good. God in his mercy numbered her with His angels at the early age of seventeen.*'

At all events, Little Nell's travels to her young demise are hotly disputed. Firstly, where exactly was the Old Curiosity Shop? Some say Portsmouth Street, near Clare Market, London. Others say just behind The National Gallery, which seems quite likely as the area Dickens describes seems to fit with its appearance in Victorian London.

As far as I can make out – with much help from others – the following was the route: St Martin's, Soho, Endell St, Tottenham Court Road and up to Hampstead. Then, hither and thither, to Warwick and the racecourse. Thereafter they wander about twelve miles to Coventry. They walk further and spend a night alongside the Warwickshire and Birmingham Canal, before arriving in Birmingham proper. They meet the schoolmaster here. By cart they proceed to Bridgenorth. Thence to Shifnal and to Tong, where Little Nell expires.

Other towns of interest in the area include Leamington Spa, where Mr Dombey comes with his new friend, the splendid Major Bagstock, in *Dombey and Son*: '*a wooden-featured, blue-faced Major, with his eyes starting out of his head… and a very rigid pair of jaw-bones, and long-flapped elephantine ears…*'

The equally splendid Mr Pickwick also travels this way en route to Birmingham, and Dickens gives us a vivid description of the city when it was a centre of industry:

'*The streets were thronged with working people. The hum of labour resounded from every house; lights gleamed from the long casement windows in the attic stories, and the whirl of wheels and noise of machinery shook the trembling walls. The fires, whose lurid, sullen light had been visible for miles, blazed fiercely up, in the great works and factories of the town. The din of hammers, the rushing of steam, and the dead heavy clanking of engines, with the harsh music which arose from every quarter*'.

11
The West Country.

Pecksniff upturned. The Fat Boy. Parents dispatched to Alphington. The fresh air of Devon and Cornwall. Lord Tennyson.

IN DICKENS' WORK, the most famous resident of Wiltshire is that pernicious hypocrite - some say based on Sir Robert Peel – Pecksniff from *Martin Chuzzlewit*. Dickens writes that he lives in a little village which is within easy travelling distance from Salisbury.

When we first meet him, he is trying to enter his house in a wind-storm. It is evident immediately that Dickens intends to give this man no peace:

'The scared leaves only flew the faster for all this, and a giddy chase it was: for they got into unfrequented places, where there was no outlet, and where their pursuer kept them eddying round and round at his pleasure; and they crept under the eaves of houses, and clung tightly to the sides of hay ricks, like bats; and tore in at open chamber windows, and cowered close to hedges; and in short went anywhere for safety. But the oddest feat they achieved was, to take advantage of the

Dickens loved to walk off his amazing energy along the coast of Cornwall, including Millendreath, Polperro, Talland Bay and The Downs. He was also very concerned with the working conditions in Cornish tin mines.

Talland Bay, near Looe
in Cornwall.

Polperro on Cornwall's South Coast.

sudden opening of Mr Pecksniff's front door, to dash wildly into his passage; whither the wind following close upon them, and finding the back door open, incontinently blew out the lighted candle held by Miss Pecksniff, and slammed the front door against Mr Pecksniff who was at that moment entering, with such violence, that in the twinkling of an eye he lay on his back at the bottom of the steps.'

Thereafter, throughout all his meanness, hypocrisy, plagiarism greed and pathos, he never ceases to make us laugh. He is ruined at the end, as both his reputation and his finances are in tatters.

The city of Exeter in Devon is famous as the place where Dickens saw an overweight boot boy when he was staying in the 15th century Turks Head Pub. He became the fat boy in *The Pickwick Papers*, at once comic and strange. He has spawned a good deal of literature

The Turk's Head in Exeter, now closed as a pub.

MILE-END COTTAGE, NEAR EXETER.

Mile End Cottage, Exeter and the slate plaque on the cottage today which commemorates this as once being the home of Dickens' parents.

among medical men right up to the present day – what exactly was wrong with him? Symptoms? He is a *'wonderfully fat boy'* and falls asleep standing up. He eats voraciously. Some experts think he had what we now call Sleep Apnea.

Also in Devon is Alphington, where Dickens dispatched his parents in 1839 – did he want to get rid of the strains they were placing upon him, and, in particular, his father's inability to stay out of debt? It is a fact that as Dickens became ever more famous, and by this time he was 27 and already a major literary star on the world stage, his father became ever more embarrassing. He would write to the wealthy and famous saying who his son was and asking for money, trusting that his son would repay them. 15 years after the young sensitive boy had been sent to Warren's Blacking Factory while his father was in debtors' prison, this latest behaviour may have been too much to bear.

He found a house – Mile End Cottage – by accident and immediately decided it was perfect, even paradise. He furnished it himself and saw to every small detail before his parents came down. He wrote the opening chapters of *Nicholas Nickleby* here and it is perhaps not surprising that Nicholas comes from nearby: throughout the novel, this part of the country is presented as a beautiful rural idyll contrasting mightily with the filth and moral squalor of the worst excesses of the city of London. Dickens' parents stayed here for four years.

Like Charles Kingsley and other writers, Dickens and his close friend, Wilkie Collins, were taken with Clovelly in North Devon, one of a handful of private villages in the UK, owned lock stock and barrel by one family since 1738. Dickens and Collins collaborated on a short story set here in 1860. It is a little convoluted and not one of their most famous. Clovelly becomes Steepway and the title of the piece is *A Message from the Sea*.

Mr Pickwick was such an excellent vehicle for a young writer because it enabled Dickens to go anywhere and comment on anything. Thus we find Mr Pickwick all over, including Somerset. Dowler and Winkle chase along the Royal Crescent in Bath and it is also here that Sam Weller, Pickwick's savvy manservant and creator of bon-mots, comments that the sea here has ' *a very strong flavour o' warm flat irons'*.

Dickens liked to escape to Devon and Cornwall on fact-finding tours, maybe seeing first hand the state of the tin mines or, more lightly, collecting material for *All the Year Round* and *Household Words*. He took Wilkie Collins with him and sometimes Forster or Maclise. One such holiday was when he was writing *David Copperfield*: the fresh air seemed to re-invigorate him and he returned to grimy old Wellington Street full of energy.

The Lizard, Cornwall became very fashionable in Victorian times, visited by a number of literary greats including Tennyson.

The railway accident, from the
Illustrated London News 1865.

The front room of Bleak House
from which Dickens would look
out across Viking Bay.

Dickens never again felt safe on trains.

There is something else to the story, too. His travelling party comprised Ellen Ternan and her mother. Dickens had met Ellen three years previously when he co-starred with her in a charity performance of *A Frozen Deep*. We have remarked earlier that when Dickens had left his wife he was very much concerned about any disapproval (and probably lessening of sales) from his adoring Victorian public. They did not approve of marriage split-ups. Even less would they have been prepared to see Dickens having a relationship with a lady many years his junior. Did he have an affair? This question has spawned a great deal of literature. Yes, he did, say some – there is even talk of a baby that died at birth. No, he didn't say others – it was just platonic. The answer is, we simply don't know.

For 24 years, Dickens visited Broadstairs with its quiet curved harbor as an idyllic escape from London. He rented Bleak House and finished *David Copperfield* there. Later he transferred his affections to Folkestone, and a house at 3 Albion Villas, because Broadstairs had become too fashionable and noisy.

Canterbury was a favourite and has a starring role in *David Copperfield*. We first hear of it from the young David, as he flees his sadistic stepfather on the way to find his Aunt Betsey. He had to hide from folk that scared him and his journey was delayed. Nevertheless, he says:

'But under this difficulty, as under all other difficulties of my journey, I seemed to be sustained and led on by my fanciful picture of my mother in my youth… It was there, among the hops, when I lay down to sleep; it was with me in my waking in the morning; it went before me all day. I have associated it ever since, with the sunny street of Canterbury, dozing as if it were in the hot light; and with the sight of its old houses and gateways, and the stately grey cathedral, with the rooks sailing round the towers.'

The Bay at Broadstairs now. Bleak House, which Dickens rented as his summer home for 22 years, can be seen high on the cliffs in the distance.

Right: In front of Canterbury Cathedral 'with rooks sailing round the towers'.

Far right: Dickens would often visit Canterbury and liked to stay at the Sun Hotel.

The West Gate and, right, The Guildhall which, prior to 1972, was the Church of the Holy Cross.

Young David eventually finds Aunt Betsey in Dover. She is gardening outside her cliff-top house. He approaches.

'Go away!' said Miss Betsey, shaking her head, and making a distant chop in the air with her knife.

'Go along! No boys here!'

I watched her, with my heart at my lips, as she marched to a corner of her garden, and stooped to dig up some little root there. Then, without a scrap of courage, but with a great deal of desperation, I went softly in and stood beside her, touching her with my finger.

'If you please, ma'am,' I began.

She started and looked up.

'If you please, aunt.'

Many of Canterbury's ancient streets lead to the cathedral, the epicentre of the city.

The House of Agnes, a few hundred yards out of the West Gate, is probably the setting for Mr Wickfield's house, the home of David Copperfield's beloved Agnes, and where David first encountered the creepy villain, Uriah Heep.

This is Guildhall Street where Dickens gave one of his famous readings, although the theatre is long gone now.

'EH?' exclaimed Miss Betsey, in a tone of amazement I have never heard approached.

'If you please, aunt, I am your nephew.'

'Oh, Lord!' said my aunt. And sat flat down in the garden-path.'

Later, after being taken in and 'officially adopted' by his kind-hearted Aunt, it is decided that young David – Aunt Betsey insists that he calls himself 'Trotwood', however – be taken to Canterbury to begin his education. Here he has his first glimpse of Uriah Heep, a man he is destined to loathe with all his being. They get out of the carriage and entered Mr Wickfield's house: *'from the window of which, I caught a glimpse, as I went in, of Uriah Heep breathing into the pony's nostrils, and immediately covering them with his hand, as if he were putting some spell upon him'.*

Weaver's Bridge, Canterbury.

You can engage a punt or a rowing boat right in the middle of the city.

114

Much more to his taste, David sees Mr Micawber – who later plays the pivotal role in the glorious undoing of Uriah Heep – in the street, which prompts Mr Micawber to exclaim:

'Walking along the street, reflecting upon the probability of something turning up (of which I am at present rather sanguine), I find a young but valued friend turn up who is connected with the most eventful period of my life; I may say, with the turning point of my existence. Copperfield, my dear fellow, how do you do?'

Probably, however, most Dickens' readers associate Kent with the legendary Dingley Dell *in The Pickwick Papers*. It is just outside Maidstone. Apparently, Dickens had been ice skating here a couple of years previously and fell through into the icy water. A most hospitable gentleman, Mr William Spong, who owned a nearby farm, came to his aid. Dickens reputedly wrote of Mr Pickwick's ice skating episodes and subsequent sumptuous happy feasts in this area as a tribute to Mr Spong's kindness.

The bustling St Peters Street – was this where David bumped into Mr Micawber?

115

13

Eastern England. Norwich-readings and elections. A very funny poem. Lowestoft. Yarmouth. Bury St Edmunds. Sudbury. Ipswich.

Acting up. Exhausting readings. A little riddle.

Dickens gives his last public reading in March 1870 as depicted by George C. Leighton in the *Illustrated London News* of that month.

IT HAS OFTEN BEEN said that Dickens' literary talent kept a great actor from the stage. Certainly, he was always fascinated by the theatre and loved to take a leading role in plays and entertainments of all sorts – we have Mamie Dickens' warm accounts of life at Gad's Hill Place where, especially when he had guests and at Christmas, all manner of entertainments would be put on. We also saw in Chapter 2, by his antics at Cooling church, how everyday life would often be turned into a performance. He also enthusiastically took part in semi-professional productions, which is how he came to meet Ellen Ternan. And, of course, he had the very greatest professional success when he wrote for the stage – witness *No Thoroughfare*, co-written with his great friend, Wilkie Collins, which wowed them at the Adelphi in the Strand.

But, of course, he also almost invented another form of entertainment as already mentioned – Readings of Charles Dickens. The theatrical nature of his prose – Mamie Dickens tells us that once she watched him at work when he was completely unaware that he was not alone: he would get up from his chair, go to the mirror and exchange conversation with his image; then he would return for a few minutes to write the exchange down, and then, hey-ho, he was up again for another one-man performance – lent itself perfectly to great dramatic monologues. Two of his most successful readings were the murder of Nancy in *Oliver Twist* and, for comedic contrast, the trial of Mr Pickwick for breach of promise.

116

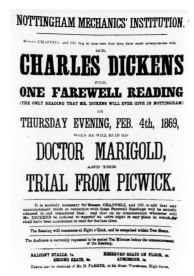

Above left: Dickens as actor: here he is cast as Captain Bobadill in *Every Man in his Humour* by Ben Johnson. He was 33 years old. *Above right:* Dickens about the time of his second tour of America.

It is not just modern artists who give 'Farewell Tours' as this poster from 1869 shows.

Inspired by Mr Pickwick's trial for breach of promise, George Cruikshank could not resist satirizing the idea of women being in charge of the judiciary. Here we see ' a contemptible scoundrel' being tried by an all-woman court. The women are knitting, chatting, eating snacks, while a huge floral centerpiece dominates the room.

Crowds gather to hear the legendary author give a reading at Steinway Hall, Boston, Massachusetts in 1867.

The people of Norwich most uncharacteristically failed to be impressed by Dickens' readings. He gave two here, one in the very grand Royal Hotel (top) and the other in the medieval monastic complex, St Andrews Hall (above) in March 1867.

These readings were to rapidly exhaust him. Afterwards, following the rapturous reception and many, many tears (from him mostly as the audience went bonkers, stomping and cheering) he could not eat, he could not sleep, he could not rest.

The readings were very popular in America. Against his doctor's advice, Dickens took a second tour of the country in 1867.

There was one place, however, where he did not do so well – Norwich. He gave two readings here – on 29 March 1867 at St Andrews Hall, a medieval monastic complex where he spoke in the main hall which bears an uncanny resemblance to the great hall at Hogwarts and is a couple of minutes walk from where this paragraph is being written at the moment; and at the Royal Hotel which (now very grand offices) was once one of the

finest hotels in Norfolk at the time which was the following day, 30 March. The audience was 'not magnetic' by which he means he could not feel any bond with the gathering. Being a native of the county, I think I can understand that Norfolk folk would possibly have been somewhat bloody-minded, determined not to be swayed by this famous author from the big smoke. We are still a bit like that, actually.

Norwich was possibly also the scene of the very funny Eatanswill elections in '*Pickwick*', where he remarks that the local people had a very fine opinion of their own importance. This is contested vigorously by several other places, notably Ipswich, but I think that the size of the election and description of the town points to Norwich.

Norwich, where Dickens' readings did not go down so well. He is reputed to have been appalled by a public hanging which he attended here, calling it 'a grotesque spectacle'. The city is also arguably the scene of the Eatanswill elections in The Pickwick Papers.

Dickens in middle age.

There is something about the city that makes it easy to imagine Dickens placing his characters here. In *English Journey*, J.B. Priestley says :"*But then to my mind, Norwich has the most Dickensian atmosphere of any city I know, except perhaps Canterbury. And this is simply due to the look of the place and not to any strong associations with Dickens.*"

It is here, too that Mr Pickwick and friends attend the summer party of Mrs Leo Hunter. My friends thought I was quite mad when, some years ago, I first read this scene: I simply kept laughing in the most unsuitable places, like the check-out queue at Marks and Spencers, as the poem arose uninvited into my mind. Mrs Leo Hunter, renowned for her literary abilities and sensitivity, has her latest work recited to an amazed Mr Pickwick. It is called '*Expiring Frog*'. It goes like this:

"Can I view thee panting, lying
On thy stomach, without sighing;
Can I unmoved see thee dying
On a log
Expiring frog!"

'*Beautiful!*' *said Mr Pickwick*

'*Fine,*' *said Mr Leo Hunter; 'so simple.*'

'*Very,*' *said Mr Pickwick.*

' *The next verse is even more touching. Shall I repeat it?*'

'*If you please,*' *said Mr Pickwick.*

'*It runs thus,*' *said the man, still more gravely.*

A caricature by André Gill of Dickens stepping over from London to Paris in 1868 when he was 56.

''Say, have fiends in shape of boys,
With wild hallo, and brutal noise,
Hunted thee from marshy joys,
With a dog,
Expiring frog!''

'Finely expressed,' said Mr Pickwick.

Great Yarmouth features in key scenes in *David Copperfield*. Dickens liked to walk here and get rid of his amazing energy. Once, in 1849, he took a holiday in Norfolk, walking from Yarmouth to Lowestoft and back again in one go – a distance of 23 miles. He found Yarmouth 'the strangest place' and set key scenes from Copperfield on an upturned boat/turned home on the beach. Little Emily was taken from here and seduced by Steerforth.

Dickens is reputed to have attended a public hanging in Norwich and was appalled at what he witnessed. They used to take place outside the Norman Castle; The Bell Hotel was a favoured place to rent a room for a good view.

Steerforth was to perish in possibly the most terrifying storm in literature, which wrecked his ship off Yarmouth sands as he attempted to return to England following his fall from grace. This is how Dickens describes it:

'The tremendous sea itself, when I could find sufficient pause to look at it, in the agitation of the blinding wind, the flying stones and sand, and the awful noise, confounded me. As the high watery walls came rolling in, and, at their highest, tumbled into surf, they looked as if the least would engulf the town. As the receding wave swept back with a hoarse roar, it seemed to scoop out deep caves on the beach, as if its purpose were to undermine the earth.'

Anthony Trollope, Dickens' famous contemporary, thought his affection for the town quite ridiculous and supposedly planned *Can You Forgive Her?* in 1863 as an antidote.

Mr Pickwick pops up all over and it is no surprise to find him in the neighbouring county of Suffolk. It is in Bury St Edmunds that he finds himself fooled – along, most unusually with the acute Sam Weller – and ends up in a compromising position in the garden of a school for young ladies.

Today, Yarmouth is a quintessential Norfolk seaside resort, but it is not hard to imagine Dickens loving the vibrancy, colour and spectacle of the present day sea front on a glorious summer's day.

The Angel Hotel, featured *in The Pickwick Papers* and also reputedly stayed in by Dickens himself. (*Portrait of Suffolk*)

Lowestoft features in David Copperfield. It is the town to which Mr Murstone, while courting Mrs Copperfield, takes young Davy for a day out. They go into a hotel and join two men who smoke cigars incessantly and occupy *'at least four chairs each.'* Later they walk on to the cliffs and then Davy is taken on board a yacht, before having a good dinner. The bonhomie is all pretence, alas, as Davy finds out to his cost after the marriage.

I have also, during the very happy researches for this account, found an interesting little riddle which concerns the Suffolk town of Ipswich. Here, Mr Pickwick, finds himself in a hotel where he gets lost looking for his room late at night. He enters a room he supposes to be his, but is mortified to find that a middle-aged lady subsequently arrives 'in yellow curl-papers'. He hides, but the lady hears a noise:

'Gracious Heaven!' said the middle-aged lady' what's that?'

'It's – it's – only a gentleman, ma-am,' said Mr Pickwick, from behind the curtains.

' A gentleman!' said the lady, with a terrific scream.

'It's all over!' thought Mr Pickwick.

' A strange man!' shrieked the lady.

Hablot Browne's engraving of the scene.

Below: A peaceful scene in Sudbury, Suffolk. *In A Passage in the Life of Mr Watkins Tott*le from *Sketches by Boz*, a young Dickens wrote of an exasperated attempt by Mr Parsons to tell a funny tale over dinner (apparently, his guests had heard in over '*four hundred times before*'): '*When I was in Suffolk,' resumed Mr. Parsons, with an impatient glance at his wife, who pretended not to observe it, 'which is now years ago, business led me to the town of Bury St. Edmund's. I had to stop at the principal places in my way, and therefore, for the sake of convenience, I travelled in a gig. I left Sudbury one dark night—it was winter time—about nine o'clock; the rain poured in torrents, the wind howled among the trees that skirted the roadside, and I was obliged to proceed at a foot-pace, for I could hardly see my hand before me, it was so dark—'*

'*John,' interrupted Mrs. Parsons, in a low, hollow voice, 'don't spill that gravy.'*

'*Fanny,' said Parsons impatiently, 'I wish you'd defer these domestic reproofs to some more suitable time. Really, my dear, these constant interruptions are very annoying.'*

To briefly complete the tale, which is quite lengthy, Mr Parsons had met a man in the road, lying down, apparently dead. However, the man had jumped up and gone on his way when Mr Parsons had approached him. Mr Parsons, somewhat miffed after all the interruptions, refuses to complete the tale, saying only that the man was apparently from a mental institution.

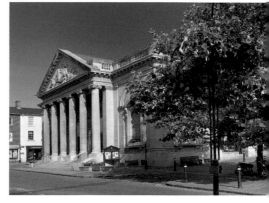

Above: The town centre of Bury St Edmunds. This is the Corn Exchange, built during Dickens' lifetime at a cost of £7000. The town witnessed the execution by hanging of William Corder in 1828 in the notorious Red Barn Murder when Corder shot his fiancée. Dickens published an account of the trial and hanging in *All The Year Round*. Dickens campaigned against such executions all his life and the aftermath of this one was particularly gruesome – you could apparently buy a piece of the hanging rope for a guinea and Corder's scalp, with an ear attached, was displayed in Oxford Street in London.

(photographs from *Portrait of Suffolk*)

123

Modern huts on the beach at Lowestoft, the scene of David Copperfield's day out with Mr Murdstone.

Pier and beach, Southwold. The seaside resort has a special link to Dickens. Southwold was the home of George Orwell and it was here that he retired, in frail health, hoping the sea air would help repair his damaged lungs. The year was 1940. Whilst here he wrote his famous essay on Charles Dickens, whom he greatly admired. He says that when he read Dickens, he saw the face of a man behind the words – *'It is the face of a man of about forty, with a small beard and a high colour. He is laughing, with a touch of anger in his laughter, but no triumph, no malignity. It is the face of a man who is always fighting against something, but who fights in the open and is not frightened, the face of a man who is generously angry…'*
(photographs from *Portrait of Suffolk*)

124

The riddle is this. *In Dickens: People and Places*, published in 1895, the author claims to have spoken to a man who has heard from another man who has spoken to Dickens himself that this is based on a real incident. It was Dickens himself who became lost in the hotel and committed this transgression. I am quite prepared to believe it, as it has the ring of truth, although the details may well have been changed for dramatic impact. It was typical of him to take and develop such a genuine incident.

It was also through Ipswich that David Copperfield comes on the night of the great storm that is to claim Steerforth's life:

'We came to Ipswich – very late, having had to fight every inch of ground since we were ten miles out of London; and found a cluster of people in the market-place, who had risen from their beds in the night, fearful of falling chimneys. Some of these, congregating about the inn-yard while we changed horses, told us of great sheets of lead having been ripped off a high church-tower, and flung into a by-street, which they then blocked up. Others had to tell of country people, coming in from neighbouring villages, who had seen great trees lying torn out of the earth, and whole ricks scattered about the roads and fields'.

Ipswich waterfront today, in tranquil mode, cannot present a starker contrast to the scenes witnessed by David in *David Copperfield*. (photographs from *Portrait of Suffolk*)

Ipswich waterfront showing (chequered building) the University Campus, Suffolk. This fine new university is proud of its Dickens connections and also has a campus in Yarmouth where key scenes in *David Copperfield* are played out. You can combine a degree course here on Literature and History.

A word about Charles Dickens and universities: Over thirty universities throughout the world now comprise '*The Dickens Project*'. This collaborative venture is based in the University of Santa Cruz and includes Yale, Stanford, California and the UK's University of Exeter.

14

Surrey, Hampshire and Sussex. Portsmouth. Isle of Wight. Brighton.

Jealous Love. Birth. Fun and games at Bonchurch. Not marrying for money. Heavenly tears.

GUILDFORD IS PROBABLY the town to which David Copperfield goes on a picnic with a party of young people. We are not absolutely sure because he was so besotted with Dora and jealous of Red Whisker that he hardly knew where he was:

'I don't know how long we were going, and to this hour I know as little where we went. Perhaps it was near Guildford. Perhaps some Arabian-night magician, opened up the place for the day, and shut it up for ever when we came away. It was a green spot, on a hill, carpeted with soft turf. There were shady trees, and heather, and, as far as the eye could see, a rich landscape.

Guildford Castle – was this where David Copperfield had his picnic in a rage of jealousy?

126

Guildford High Street.

Charles Dickens

'It was a trying thing to find people here, waiting for us; and my jealousy, even of the ladies, knew no bounds. But all of my own sex – especially one impostor, three or four years my elder, with a red whisker, on which he established an amount of presumption not to be endured – were my mortal foes.

We all unpacked our baskets, and employed ourselves in getting dinner ready. Red Whisker pretended he could make a salad (which I don't believe), and obtruded himself on public notice. Some of the young ladies washed the lettuces for him, and sliced them under his directions. Dora was among these. I felt that fate had pitted me against this man, and one of us must fall.'

Glorious Chichester, dominated by the Cathedral.

Portsmouth is famous as the place of Charles Dickens' birth – in Mile End Terrace. The family moved often thereafter during the first five years of his life: we know that they moved to Hawk Street, Wish Street and finally to 22 Cleveland Street (10 Norfolk Street now). His father worked in the Naval Pay Office just inside the gates of Portsmouth Dockyard – the building is still there – finally leaving for good in 1817 when Charles was five years old. He never came back there to live, and the city of his birth features very little in his novels. These early years held no great affection for him, perhaps.

Just across the water, though, is somewhere of which he was very fond – the Isle of Wight. This is linked to one of the most productive periods in his life. In 1850 he was finishing his 'favourite child', *David Copperfield*, and had decided to launch *Household Words*. Everything was going fantastically well – he was, at 38, a world-famous name and in very rude health. He hopped about all over the place: London, Broadstairs, Paris and, notably, Bonchurch on the island, where he spent a very happy summer. Bathing (in cold water, which he believed most health-inducing), putting on plays and walking long distances with his super-fast stride, he seems to have had one of the happiest times of his life. Locals were amazed, some favourably and some definitely not, at this man who was excessively full of himself. Some would pass him in the street and then double back to take another look. Never one for subtleties in his manner or his flamboyant dress sense, he was spotted with his entourage by Thackeray on the pier at Ryde. Thackeray thought him 'abominably coarse' but, infuriatingly to Thackeray, one feels, very happy.

It is then no surprise to find that he sets one of his famous comic scenes on the island – on Shanklin Sands. In *Our Mutual Friend*, Mr Lammie has just married Sophronia, both of them under the impression that the other is rich. They discover their mutual error whilst strolling on the beach:

"After a little more walking and a little more silence, Mr Lammie breaks the latter.

"You shall proceed in your own way. You claim a right to ask me do I mean to tell you. Do I mean to tell you what?'

Vicars Row, Chichester.

'That you are a man of property?'

'No.'

'Then you married me on false pretences?'

' So be it. Next comes what you mean to say. Do you mean to say you are a woman of property?'

'No.'

' Then you married me on false pretences.'"

As regards an idyllic place to visit, to watch Dickens being performed, it is hard to beat Chichester Festival Theatre. The city itself is in the form of a cross and dominated by the Cathedral, which is nearly a thousand years old. It is free to enter, open every day of the year, and has a lovely café in the Cloisters. Many theatre-lovers, including my own family, will meet here on a summer evening before strolling up to the theatre itself. It was opened in 1962 and the first Artistic Director was Sir Laurence Olivier. There was much excitement in 2006 at the eight-hour revival of *Nicholas Nickelby*.

Dickens is possibly most famous in most people's minds for his untiring life-long campaign for what we today might call 'children's rights'. This had to do with the way society, including oftentimes their own parents, let them down and abused them – witness, famously, Wackford Squeers, workhouses employing the likes of Mr Bumble, and the fate of Little Nell. In nearby Brighton he stages a scenario that had the Victorian world in tears – the neglect and death of little Paul Dombey.

Mr Dombey, who sees his frail son as simply an extension of his own glory, sends him down to Brighton and to the 'school', if it can so laughingly be termed, of the *'ogress and child-queller'*, Mrs Pipchin:

'This celebrated Mrs Pipchin was a marvellous ill-favoured, ill-conditioned old lady, of a stooping figure, with a mottled face, like bad marble, a hook nose, and a hard grey eye, that looked as if it might have been hammered at on an anvil without sustaining any injury. Forty years at least had elapsed since the Peruvian mines had been the death of Mr Pipchin; but his relict still wore black bombazeen, of such a lusterless, deep, dead, sombre shade, that gas itself couldn't light her up after dark, and her presence was a quencher to any number of candles. She was generally spoken of as a 'great manager' of children; and the secret of her management was, to give them everything that

they didn't like, and nothing that they did – which was found to sweeten their dispositions very much. She was such a bitter old lady, that one was tempted to believe there had been some mistake in the application of the Peruvian machinery, and that all her waters of gladness and milk of human kindness, had been pumped out dry, instead of the mines.'

Paul soon transferred to Dr Blimber's establishment. This was not malign, just cold, inflexible and heartless, the Principal himself being a tragi-comic creation of pure pomposity.

His mesmerized public watched in horror as Dickens made Paul, tended by his adoring and adorable sister, Floy, fade away little by little. The press was full of speculation as to whether Dickens could possibly let Paul go altogether: should he, could he, will he, won't he, can he? Yes, he can:

'Now lay me down,' he said, 'and, Floy, come close to me, and let me see you!'

Sister and brother wound their arms around each other, and the golden light came streaming in, and fell upon them, locked together.

'How fast the river runs, between its green banks and the rushes, Floy! But it's very near the sea. I hear the waves! They always said so!'

He gains a vision of his Mother.

'Mama is like you, Floy. I know her by the face! But tell them that the print upon the stairs at school is not divine enough. The light about the head is shining on me as I go!'

The golden ripple on the wall came back again, and nothing else stirred in the room. The old, old fashion! The fashion that came in with our first garments, and will last unchanged until our race has run its course, and the wide firmament is rolled up like a scroll. The old, old fashion – Death!'

There was hardly a dry eye in the English speaking world but, for a few unworthy souls it has to be said, the tears shed were tears of laughter.

15

What Now? Please love me.

Getting the family involved. A suggested sequence of reading. Will you love me?

LOOKING AT THE VAST collection of Dickens' work, it can be difficult to know where to start. These are a few ideas to get started.

If you have children, how about taking it in turns to sit around the living room and read aloud the whole of *A Christmas Carol*? It is short and will take maybe three hours. It is very funny and heartwarming, but as it will make you hungry when Dickens talks of Christmas fare (which is often), it is a good idea to have some snacks, nuts, fruit and things to nibble.

Dickens receiving his characters, an illustration by William Holbrook Beard.

It is also the most perfect novel ever written. There is not an excess word. Here we have Charles Dickens in his pomp. He read it aloud to Maclise, Forster, Wilkie Collins and his family. I see him, with a glint in his eye, settling everyone down after dinner, saying, *'I have written something. Care to hear it?'* He would have thoroughly enjoyed himself, watching all their faces. Then, at the end, silence. What could they say?

Next, you could try Dickens' own favourite, *David Copperfield*. This is very much based on his own life and so is especially interesting. It also has one of the great comic creations of the age, Mr Micawber, who is always waiting for something to 'turn up'. In Uriah Heep, we

Oliver Twist in trouble at the undertakers' by George Cruikshank.

A wonderful engraving by an unknown artist showing Mr Pickwick and Sam Weller pointing out Dickens' literary characters.

have one of the strangest – he creeps up on you throughout the novel - villains in literature. And what do you make of Steerforth, Dickens' 'Black Angel' ? He is at once charming, intelligent, handsome, insightful – he names David Copperfield 'Daisy' on account of his fresh and open nature – and, ultimately, morally flawed. The jury is still out on this one.

Third has to be *Oliver Twist*, possibly the most famous novel he ever wrote. For sheer villainy, it is hard to beat Sikes: his murder of Nancy was the most popular of Dickens' readings. Will you have just a twinge of sympathy for Fagin?

After all the drama around young Oliver, you may appreciate the hilarity of *The Pickwick Papers* and, especially, the ploys and plans of Mr Pickwick's manservant and rescuer on many occasions, Sam Weller. After a slow start, with the introduction of Sam, the book's sales reached unprecedented levels and it is good to read the book that made Dickens a very famous young man all around the world, and a permanent superstar in the literary firmament.

Then you could have a go at *Dombey & Son.* I once lent this to a friend who was an accountant and who had not read any Dickens before and he recorded that he cried exactly sixteen times during the book! The death of young Paul Dombey caused a mass outbreak of Victorian grief.

Great Expectations, Nicholas Nickleby, Martin Chuzzlewit, Our Mutual Friend and the rest await and, by now, you are bound to be 'hooked' and will need no nudging from me to start them.

A friend asked me ' Why not start with *Sketches by Boz?* Isn't this the obvious place to start? It was his first book. ' Well, no, actually. Compared with what comes later, it lacks a certain something. Some of it is indeed fantastic, but also Dickens is struggling in other parts. He was trying to establish his style. He wrote this and then accepted the commission to do *'Pickwick'*, and that, too, did not really 'take off' for the first few chapters; but *when* it did, oh my goodness, *how* it did!

A final enjoyable idea for the family is to read the last, great, unfinished novel, *The Mystery of Edwin Drood,* and then to finish it verbally or in writing. This has been done by many people in print, some more successfully than others. Dickens wrote the final words on the day before he died, but I think he is smiling somewhere as he loved puzzles and he left this big one for us to work out for ourselves.

From first to last, Charles Dickens craved public recognition. It killed him in the end. This phenomenally energetic man with the bright waistcoats and the greatest literary talent since Shakespeare would like you to love him.

Will you not?

Appendix - A conversation

IT WAS ON A CLASSIC balmy summer's evening that the idea occurred. Phoebe, Freddie and I were sitting, drink in hand, watching the swans gliding up and down the Serpentine in Hyde Park. The conversation meandered around to what you would like to say to any famous person, alive or not, if you were granted an audience. Then, after another drink, it seemed only natural to ask the barman for some paper and pens and we all sat in silence (occasional half-suppressed guffaws apart) for about half an hour, scribbling away.

Freddie chose to take Proust to task, but it was all a bit philosophical for me. Phoebe chatted to her beloved John Keats, although it was a shame she could only remember two lines of *Endymion* on this particular evening. Naturally, as his number one fan, I chose Charles Dickens. I told him I was feeling a bit annoyed with him because, if only he had managed to slow down a little, he would have lived longer, finished *The Mystery of Edwin Drood* and given us many more delights. I told him this, and he said:

'How dare you talk about me like that, Stephen?'

'Why, what is the problem?'

'You are not as respectful as I would wish. Have you written any books?'

'Yes, about sixteen, Mr Dickens'.

'Are they any good?'

'Not as good as yours.'

' Naturally. I touched people's hearts. Like your Princess Diana, I was the people's author'.

'And very good you were at it, too. Shame about…'

'Shame about what?'

'Well, shame about your unnecessary melodrama sometimes. And you don't like women, do you?'

'I had ten children – how do you think I did that?'

'I won't say. What I mean is that you seem much more successful at creating a complex male character – say, Steerforth or David Copperfield – than an interesting woman. Err…your young ladies, well, they are all sort of…very correct, aren't they? Either good or comically bad. Not like Thackeray's Becky Sharp. A bit immoral, a bit sexy, very capable - all at the same time…'

' Don't talk to me of Thackeray! Anyway, a real Victorian gentleman doesn't talk about such things as women's complex needs and personalities.'

'A 21st century one does. Anyway, I am very angry with you, too'.

'You impertinent little scamp'

'Scamp??'

'Yes. In my time it means someone who does not know his place'.

'Whatever..'

'What?'

'Whatever – it means basically shut up and listen. Why did you kill yourself? You had it all. Money. Fame. As much as J K Rowling and Harry Potter. You are a kind of Dumbledore as regards the English language – wonderful, magical, moral, mesmeric…'

'Who?'

'Never mind. I am angry because you do not take any rest. It is 1870. Queen Victoria meets you – people think she might have offered you a knighthood behind closed doors. That would have been nice, wouldn't it? Then you could have relaxed at Gad's Hill and written the ending to Edwin Drood.'

The young Catherine Dickens – sometimes Charles became annoyed as she lacked his phenomenal energy.

'I don't want any honour. I am the people's champion – my street cred would be ruined…'

'Like Sir Winston Churchill, you mean – he refused further honours and was concerned about his 'cred', too'.

'Who?'

'He is a British hero'.

'Not as big as me, tho', surely.'

'Yes, I am sorry to say even bigger than you'.

' Unbelievable. What did he do?'

'He saved world civilisation'.

'Whatever – becoming used to your 21st century words. Hmm…I am getting a bit mellow now. Give me a cigar and a glass of what you are drinking. Churchill seems like a fine chap. Like to meet him. Anyway, David – that is your name, I think – what are you doing now?'

'Stephen…'

'What?'

'My name is Stephen. But I won't take any offence! At the moment I am writing a book about you.'

' Excellent! That Thackeray chap, he wasn't too bad but I never got the chance to tell him so. I am sorry. He died on me. And my good friend, Wilkie Collins, how is he doing in the 21st century?'

'Thackeray is reputed to be a great alongside you – not as great as you, of course – but Wilkie is struggling. His books are in our bookshops, but people don't rate him. This will change'.

'And you are writing a book about me, Eh? Is it all good?'

'No, 'fraid not. You have genius but I want to shake you to stop you exhausting and killing yourself'.

A portrait by a contemporary of Dickens' artist Charles Green. It is of Florence Dombey and her friend and benefactor, Captain Cuttle. In a scene of perfect friendly tranquility, Florence is a saintly figure – she even has a light shining before her.

'I don't want to stop. Don't stop me now'.

'Like Freddy Mercury?'

'Who? What?'

'He was a singer from the group 'Queen'. He said that, too.'

'Groups of Queens? Are you ruled by several people? Absurd. And how is the mighty Empire which my illustrious Queen Victoria ruled over (God Bless Her)?'

'Gone, I am afraid – poof! In a mere micro-second of history. America rules now. Then it will be China or maybe India. Every nation seems to have its time in the sun, don't you think?'.

'That is quite ridiculous. Can't we send a gunship to sort things out? Re-establish the old order?'

An unfinished painting by Robert W. Buss of Dickens, in Gad's Hill Place, dreaming of his characters.

'No, but we can use you to show how things can be maybe cleared up – your expressions, your intonations, your genius for language…An awful lot of problems could be sorted with clearer, more imaginative communication.'

'And you will make these skills of mine clear in this book you are writing about me?'

'I will try, sir, I will try'.

'Then you have my blessing.'

'Thank you, Mr Dickens'.

'You are very welcome. This wine is not at all bad, eh? Give me another glass. Now, what was your name again?'

'Please sir, I want some more.'